Sweet Baby Lover

SWEET BABY LOVER

A true story of love, death, and hope

Jule Kucera

Poppyseed House

Poppyseed House
Published by Poppyseed House
5847 Crain Street, Morton Grove, Illinois 60053, U.S.A.

Much of this book first appeared on the author's website, www.julekucera.com.

From No Death, No Fear by Thich Nhat Hanh, copyright © 2002 by the Unified Buddhist Church. Used by permission of Riverhead Books, an imprint of Penguin Group (USA) LLC.

From The Places You Go blogpost by Seth Godin, copyright © 2010 by Seth Godin. Used with permission.

Trent Price photograph by Jule Kucera.
Author photograph by Kendra Cribley.

Printed in the United States of America
Set in Palatino nova with Alright Sans, Moon Flower
ISBN 978-0-9904555-0-9 (Pbk)

For the eight women who carried me

Ginger and Laura

Laurie and Linda

Denise and Sabine

Kendra and Elaine

Trent Price, March 2007

I wish I could wrap you up like a cocoon so I could hold you from all around and be loving you. Then you could be a butterfly every morning.

—Trent Price

Author's Note

This is a true story, or as true as I can tell it. It is inherently flawed in that it is my perspective and that it is told in hindsight. My commitment to you is to tell the story as honestly as I can. I will not change the facts to influence your opinion of someone; I will not change what happened to make the story more interesting. Real names are used most of the time. When the name is a pseudonym, it is marked with an asterisk the first time it is used.

Others would no doubt tell the story differently. But this is my story and this is my truth.

Prologue

If you are one of those people who likes to know how the story turns out before you decide to settle in with it or not, if you want to know in advance whether the hero lives or dies, here's the answer: he dies.

This doesn't mean this story has a sad ending, however. For one thing, the story isn't over yet. For another, the hero dying might not be an entirely bad thing. A hard thing, a grievous thing, a thing I never asked for or wanted, yes, all those are true. But a bad thing? I can't say that.

COMING TOGETHER

1. The Beginning

June 2003

Although the real estate agent had said, "Parking is never a problem," parking was frequently a problem. I stood on the upstairs back enclosed porch of my Chicago two-flat—what Chicagoans call a two-story two-unit residence with a common front door—and decided that part of the backyard needed to be sacrificed. I needed to find someone to tear down the weathered wood stockade fence that separated the backyard from the alley, then pour a concrete parking pad, and then build a new wood fence on the near side of the new parking pad. The mounds of perennials planted by the previous owners would be given away or thrown away—they were part of a cottage garden that wasn't my style. The small redbud tree could be moved.

I called Jane* to get the name of the guy who had done the rehab on her three-flat. She said, "Nobody can do concrete better than Trent, and nobody in Chicago can beat his price." I called him—it was a Michigan phone number—and we made an appointment for a Saturday.

July 2003

He was late, more than an hour late. I was walking back and forth in the kitchen, declaring all contractors unreliable, doing mental calculations of where I might find somebody if this guy didn't work out. The doorbell rang and I tore down the twisting front stairway, deciding whether to be mad that he was late or glad that he was finally here. When I pulled open the heavy door, he was framed in sunlight. He wasn't what I expected. He was beautiful.

He wore a yellow T-shirt, heavy canvas shorts, work boots, and thick socks with the top rolled down so that the fuzzy part showed. He was tall and broad-shouldered, with blond hair that shone in the sun, a blond beard flecked with white, and blue eyes that were smiling at me. I smiled back.

He said his name was Trent. I said mine was Jule. We then walked through the side alley to the backyard, talking about what needed to be done. I said I would dig out and move the redbud. He said he would take care of the rest. We talked about the dimensions of the parking pad and how thick the concrete needed to be to withstand the winter and the weight of the vehicles. I explained that I needed room to park two cars—a space for me and a space for the downstairs tenants.

He asked what I wanted the fence to look like. I remembered a fence that I had spotted while walking my dog, Charlie, a graying standard poodle that I had rescued from Texas. Trent and I walked to where I thought it was but couldn't find it at first—I had gotten confused about which street it was on—but he was patient.

The bottom half of the fence was solid, the boards alternately projected and recessed. In the top half, every other board was removed. I liked the top—it nicely mingled the lightness of the air above with the solidity of the wood beneath. I was pretty sure he was going to tell me that the style was too difficult or would cost a lot more when he said, "This shouldn't be too hard," and asked me to hold the tape measure so he could measure it. I took the end of the tape down to the bottom of the fence, putting myself at eye level with his calves. I looked at his muscles (the gastrocnemius) at the back of his calves and how they were thick and angled at the bottom rather than rounded. I looked at his tanned skin and the blond curly hair that ran from the top of his socks to up under his shorts. He said, "Okay, I got it," and it was time for me to stand up and let go of the tape. I didn't want to.

August 2003

He came back a few weeks later, driving a 1980s Chevy truck that had mellowed to a soft blue. I stood on the upstairs back porch, sometimes leaving to do other things but most of the time watching him and hoping that the reflection of the sun off the porch windows made me difficult to see.

He had a heavy chain he attached to the back of his truck, the other end to part of the fence. When he stepped on the gas, the truck moved forward, the chain unfurled, then snapped straight, the truck lurched, the section of fence came down, the brakes screeched, and the truck stopped abruptly. Accelerate-jerk-slam, over and over. It was tricky because the alley was only a few feet wider than the truck.

There were actually two fences to deal with. The wood stockade fence bordered the alley and a chain-link fence ran alongside it, on the house side. After both fences were down, I realized that we also had to contend with an out-of-commission telephone pole, naked now that the fences were sprawled at its feet.

Trent backed the truck up to the telephone pole. I watched his shoulder muscles work—he had taken off his T-shirt—as he wrapped the chain around the tall pole. Accelerate-jerk-slam, again and again until the pole wobbled. He got out of the truck and pushed on the pole. It tilted but wouldn't fall. He got back in the truck and jerk-slammed it a few more times, but the pole stayed where it was. At this point, he squatted down, wrapped his arms around the pole, and lifted it out of the ground. He turned slightly and let the pole fall in the alley, away from his truck. I may have gasped.

He told me he was going to the dump. (How did he tell me this? Had he hollered up to me? Had I gone down to offer him something to drink?) I disappeared into the house. When I looked out the porch window a few minutes later, the wooden fence was gone and the truck was gone, but the chain-link fence was lying in the alley and I was angry again. Why didn't he take both fences at the same time? Both would have fit in the truck. He was being paid hourly—was he just trying to make the job take longer?

As I stood there, an old pickup truck with plywood sheets affixed to both sides of the truck bed pulled up and stopped. Three small men got out of the truck, picked up the fence, threw it in the back of the truck, and drove away. "Scrappers,"

Trent said when I told him about it later. "They come through about every twenty minutes." A booming business in Chicago, he explained. He offered to take me over to the scrap yard if I wanted to see it but warned me that it was kind of scary—a *Mad Max Beyond Thunderdome* kind of place. I declined.

The Bobcat

The next Saturday, Trent brought a friend with him. The previous owners, Trent told me, had brought in a lot of soil for their flowerbeds. The extra dirt had changed the drainage—the backyard now sloped toward the house and water drained into the basement. This explained why I heard the sump pump running every time I went down to the basement to do laundry.

The two of them shoveled dirt into the back of the truck all day Saturday and all day Sunday. Sunday evening I looked out the window but couldn't see much of a difference.

On Monday, I came home from work to see a little Bobcat (the earthmoving equipment, not the animal) in the backyard, Trent driving it, picking up a load of dirt in the front bucket, then spinning around to drop the dirt in the bed of his pickup. He seemed to be having a good time. I watched them, the man and the machine, mesmerized. They looked like they were dancing together across the dirt. I wanted to take a picture but didn't want to be embarrassed if he caught me. I walked outside instead.

Trent apologized for not asking before renting the Bobcat but said it was the only way to get the dirt dug before the ground froze. Chicago is built on a swamp and its soil is heavy clay that sticks to every shovelful. It is a backbreaker.

When he stopped for the night, I looked out the back window and saw the Bobcat resting by the neighbor's garage. This time I did take a picture. The slope of the ground appeared to be changing but I still couldn't tell for sure. The alley was tightly lined with fences and garages, except for my backyard. There was nothing between my two-flat and the alley. I felt exposed. I felt vulnerable.

The next day when I came home from work and looked out the window, I could see the difference in the ground. It sloped away from the house and ended at the alley, a few inches below the asphalt. Trent was just finishing nailing bright-orange plastic webbing to 2×4s planted in a row where the future fence would be. I walked outside and he said, "I thought this might make you feel a little safer, until the real one is up."

We talked about the exact dimensions of the parking pad, how it should meet the asphalt of the alley, and the grade of concrete he should use. I hadn't known that concrete came in different grades and accepted his recommendation.

After he said he wanted to show me something on the side of the house, we clambered over the low chain-link fence that blocked the side yard. A climbing vine had crawled up the brick, and Trent said the vine should come down, explaining what I was vaguely aware of, that the vine puts its climbing feet into the brick and damages it.

Trent climbed back over the fence and held out his hand to help me over. As he pulled me over, I felt a powerful wave go from his hand to my hand through my entire body. When I got over the fence, he let go and all I wanted was for him to hold my hand again, to touch me, for me to feel his hand again, to feel that wave. I held out my hands to show him how green they were from pulling down the vine, hoping that he would touch me again but he didn't even look. I let them fall.

Concrete

Trent and his friend Paul were just finishing up pouring the concrete for the parking pad when I got home. The orange netting of the temporary fence was down on the ground, waiting to be put back up when the concrete was finished.

A few minutes later, my next-door neighbor Jim got home from his construction job and also came outside. Jim and I had been on uneasy terms ever since I had moved in, when repairs to my roof had, he said, covered the inside of his place with a fine layer of soot, including his best dress shirt that had been laid out, he said, in preparation for a special evening.

He stood there in his T-shirt with cut-off sleeves, his long light-brown hair pulled back in a thin ponytail, his eyes surveying the operation. Jim will tell you, as he told Trent, that he is an ex-Marine. Trent will tell you that Jim is also bit ADHD. When Jim saw that the pour was complete, his shoulders drooped a bit. Trent told Jim that he could help with brushing the surface but that they would have to wait about an hour or so, given the humidity. This reenergized Jim and his feet began to shift on the ground.

Paul asked if they could put their names in the concrete and Trent said yes, in the corner he pointed to, where they had started the pour. Paul went first. Trent added his name and 2003. Then Paul asked whether, since Jim was there, he could leave so that he could go into the city. Jim would take over for Paul, who was gone so fast I almost didn't see him leave.

Trent and Jim discussed brushing the concrete, the brush they would use, and the extender pole, and how they would work together to do it. This got Jim excited. "Let's brush it now, man."

"If we do that, the brushing won't hold. We need it to firm up first."

"No man, it will be okay. Look—it's stiff enough already." As Jim moved to touch the concrete, Trent stopped him.

"Nope. Not yet. It will lose the brush marks."

"So what, man. You don't really need those. Those are for appearances. We'll smooth it out and call it a day."

"Smooth isn't good—not when it's wet or snowed on."

Jim's feet started shifting faster and you could see just how hard it was going to be for him to wait, which is when Trent turned to me and spoke in a voice low enough for Jim not to hear.

"Can you talk to him for a few minutes while I go get something? When I get back, you can go inside and you won't have to be out here with him anymore. Just don't let him touch that brush."

Trent then turned to Jim. "Hey man, I want to go get us some-thing. I'll be right back."

Then Trent was gone and I was standing next to my neighbor. I needed to change his focus and get him talking about something else, quickly.

"So, Trent tells me you were in the Marines?"

It was enough. Jim was still talking when Trent walked up the alley a while later with a six-pack hanging from each hand. I went inside and heard them talking and laughing for a long while, until it was almost dark and there was just enough light left to brush the concrete, which is when Trent finally let Jim pick up the brush.

The next day when I got home from work, I went to my usual perch on the back porch. Trent was cutting boards for the fence. He would place a board on his table saw and then slice it with the blade, sawdust swirling in the sunlight. It was hot and he was sweating and the sawdust was sticking to him and the sun was glinting off the sawdust. He looked like a great golden bear. I watched how he held the boards, how he felt the weight of them, how he measured them, how his strong hands carried and placed them carefully. I wanted to trade places with those boards. I wanted him to carry me and place me carefully.

The Drill

Trent was assembling the fence, attaching the vertical boards to the horizontal stringers he had placed earlier. I walked outside, told him that I had my own cordless drill, and asked if I could help. I was proud of my drill. After my divorce five years earlier, I had gone to the hardware store to replenish my left-behind tools. I had picked up flat- and Phillips-head screwdrivers, a hammer, a tape measure, and a short level. A salesman had approached as I eyed the wall of drills—some corded, most cordless.

"So, you're looking for a drill?"

"Yes. I am."

"What kind of drill are you looking for?"

"I'm not sure."

"Well, what do you want to use it for?"

"Basic stuff around the house, like hanging up shelves. Stuff like that."

"Okay. Well, there are a lot here that'll do that for you."

"Really, it just needs to be better than the one my ex-husband has."

"What does he have?"

"A Makita."

"Well, then. You need a DeWalt."

I stood next to Trent with my 12-volt DeWalt and helped screw in screws to build the fence. He stood nearby with his 18-volt DeWalt. He never got mad when I slipped off a screw or drove one crooked, and he showed me how to lean on the end of the drill (drill motor, he called it) to make the screw go in straight and quick.

It got late and I got hungry. I told Trent that I was going to get some dinner and asked him whether he wanted any. I hoped he did, of course.

We sat upstairs on the back porch and ate falafel and rice. He was easy to talk to. He had a nice laugh and crinkles at the corners of his eyes when he smiled. It got dark and I suddenly felt stupid—pining after the man who was building my fence and making him have dinner with me. Could he honestly have said no? I felt guilty and embarrassed and told him that it was getting late. We both stood up. As I watched his back move down the stairs, I noticed a slump in his shoulders and for the first time thought that maybe he had been having a good time, too. I wanted to say I was sorry and I wanted to be left alone and I didn't want to be hurt and I wanted him to hold me.

2. Five Years

September 2003

"I haven't had sex in five years."

I said this to Persephone after I sat down at the back corner of the classroom where we were to observe a new training program. I hadn't even said hello first.

Persephone is one of those people who takes things in stride. She looked at me with a steady face—no shock, no surprise, no discomfort with the topic—and said, "That's not good." When the program ended, we went straight to her office: me desperate to solve the problem; Persephone determined to help me.

She asked, "Do you have any friends?"

"Sure, I have friends."

"No, that's not what I meant. Do you have any friends . . . with benefits?"

"With benefits?"

"With benefits."

She leaned in closer and clarified. "Friends who would be interested in participating with you to end your 'no sex in five years' problem."

"Oh."

Persephone smiled. She let the wheels turn in my head until my eyes widened and I asked, "Do people do that?"

"Yes, they do."

"Really?"

"Really. In fact, I may have done such a thing myself. So, can you think of any friends in that category?"

"Hmmm . . . No."

"No? None?"

"Well, there's this one guy. He's not really a friend, but. . ."

"But he might be interested?"

"He might."

"There you go."

"There I go what? What do I do, just walk up to him and say, 'Hey, do you want to have sex?'"

"You could do that."

"No, I couldn't. I really couldn't."

We agreed that verbalizing my request might be too much for me and that a written note might be better. I didn't know what to write but Persephone gave me the first line: "How do you feel about casual sex?" I finished the rest of it, ending with "If you're interested, let's talk. If not, please throw this note away and never mention it."

I waited before I gave him the note—I wanted a safety check before proceeding. My therapist thought it was a splendid idea. I decided to give it to him on a Friday. If he wasn't interested, he would be in Michigan for the weekend and I would have two days to hide and feel stupid.

On Thursday night, I took out my favorite cream-colored stationery with the rag edges and wrote the note several times. The first few versions were to get the spacing of the words right on the page. The next few were to work some unsteadiness out of the script. I got it as nice-looking as I could.

On Friday morning, I took out the note, reread the words, put it in a matching cream-colored/rag-edged envelope, wrote his name on the front, and put it in his toolbox. Then I left.

Friday, October 3, 2003

I was worthless at work. I went to meetings, spoke when spoken to, and did what I needed to do to appear to be functioning. My body was present but my mind was on a cream-colored note sitting in a large toolbox inside the downstairs back door of a two-flat.

People at work knew something was up. I was wearing a short black leather skirt, chunky black sweater, black tights, and little black heels. They were used to seeing me in blue jeans and a blazer. I didn't say a word. They didn't ask.

By the time I got to The "L," Chicago's mostly aboveground subway system that would carry me home, I was nearly dizzy. My brain had spent the day considering every possible response he might have and all of my possible reactions. I was exhausted. I wanted to stay on that train and ride it past Rockwell, past the end of the line at Kimball, past Wisconsin, into Canada. Canada sounded good.

I got off The "L" at Rockwell and walked the two blocks home. Trent wasn't waiting for me by the front door, however. That was Ideal Scenario #1. I unlocked the door, walked upstairs, unlocked my door, and put down my work things. I couldn't hear any sound coming from the back—no sawing, no drilling, nothing. Maybe he had fled—that was another of the possible outcomes that had whistled through my head. I went down the back stairs and found him in the backyard. He said there were some things he wanted to show me. It was cold outside and I wrapped my arms tightly around myself for warmth and self-bolstering.

He was talking about some aspect of the fence but I could hardly hear him. All I could think about was the note that he wasn't talking about. As he walked me from the fence to the back of the house to show me something that needed to be repaired, I saw his mouth move but heard nothing. I wanted to melt, dissolve, sink between the blades of dry grass and gray dirt. I wanted to disappear. I stood there in my little black heels and wanted to die.

This is when he said, "Do you want to talk?"

"What?"

"Do you want to talk?"

"Oh. Talk?"

"Yes. Talk. Do you want to?"

"Uh. Yes."

"It would probably be good if we could sit down somewhere."

"The back porch?"

"Sounds good."

I led the way up the back stairs and hoped he thought I had nice legs.

We sat down at the corner of the table on the back porch, me with my back to the house, Trent to my right, facing me.

"Does Jane know?" he asked.

Jane, my friend who had recommended him for the work? Of all the things I had imagined he might say, this was not one of them.

"Does Jane know what?"

"Does Jane know about the letter you put in my tools?"

"No, Jane doesn't know."

"I thought the two of you might have talked about it."

I remembered back to the phone conversation Jane and I had a few weeks earlier, where Jane was complaining about the lack of good men in the world.

"What about Trent?" I had said to Jane.

"Trent?"

"Yeah, Trent. He seems like a nice guy."

"I'm not interested."

"Why not? He's cute."

"I'm not interested in Trent."

"Well if you're not, then maybe I am."

"I wouldn't recommend it."

"Why not?"

"Because he's a drunk, he's broke, and he has a terrible temper."

"Really?"

"Yep. I've known him for years. He's not a guy you want to date."

"Then maybe I shouldn't have him work on my backyard."

"No, he'll do a good job at that. I just wouldn't date him."

"I don't know if I want to hire him."

"He's not going to be drinking on the job. He does really good work and he's cheap."

I managed to pull myself back into the present and the conversation with Trent.

"No. Why would I tell Jane?"

"You just might have."

"Well, I didn't. And why would she care, anyway?"

"Because Jane and I are seeing each other."

It felt as if the chair beneath me had been pulled away and I had fallen to the floor—my butt on the terra-cotta tiles, my feet stretched out in front of me.

"You're seeing each other?"

"We have been."

"For how long?"

"Five years."

Five years! I did the math. Five years included the ten-day vacation Jane and I had taken together in Greece, when we sailed in a boat while the world watched two tall buildings and people falling down against a bright blue sky. After that Tuesday, Jane called someone almost every day and wouldn't tell me whom she was calling. Toward the end of the trip, she gave way a bit and said, "Just an old friend from Michigan."

On that trip, when I'd complained about my nonexistent love life, Jane told me that she was content because she was quite good at self-pleasure; she said nothing about a tall blond man from Michigan. She suggested that I improve my personal-pleasure skills.

For the first part of the conversation with Trent, then, I was not really there. I was on the floor, I was on vacation with Jane, I was once again feeling stupid. *Focus*, I told myself. *Focus*.

At this point, Trent asked if I minded if he had a beer. I said no. He pulled two blue cans from the kangaroo pocket of his camouflage sweatshirt and set them on the table. He snapped one open and began to talk again. "It's been a rough day for me. I thought she might have pimped me out."

"What?"

"I thought Jane might have pimped me out."

"To me?"

"Yes."

"Oh, no. No."

He let go of a long breath and looked out the window for a while. Looking at the redness in his face, I realized that there had been several beers ahead of the two on the table.

He spoke again. "What do you want to do?"

I thought about it. I had propositioned the boyfriend of what I had thought was a good friend of mine—a boyfriend she had never told me about.

"I'd like to keep talking."

He took a draw on his beer. "So would I."

I paused a minute and asked, "How would you feel about cheating on Jane with me?"

"I think it's fair."

"What makes it fair?"

"I'm pretty sure I'm not her only, so she doesn't need to be mine."

He looked sad when he said it and I wondered if he loved her.

The next thing he did was pull out his keychain, thumbing through the keys until he came to a plastic tab with a photo on it. He held it out toward me.

"This is my daughter, Jenna. Jenna Jo."

I was on the floor again. Jane had told me he had a daughter. "He's a good father," was one of the things she had said when persuading me to hire him. But in all my reveries about Trent, I had left out his daughter. I quickly included her into the rapidly expanding circle: Trent, Jane, me, and Jenna.

"She's beautiful."

I have learned that this is what you should say when you see a picture of someone's daughter, no matter what you really think. It was hard to tell what Jenna looked like—the plastic tab was badly scratched. The photo had rubbed away in many places and white was showing through. Trent smiled.

"She's a sweetheart."

"She looks darling."

"She's older now—older than the picture."

"How old?"

"She's ten."

"How old is she in the picture?"

"Five."

Trent looked sad again and I thought I should change the subject. I groped for a new conversation topic and came up with nothing but a question.

"So what else should we talk about?"

"What we're not talking about."

"Yes."

He paused and I said nothing, so he said, "You want to have sex with me."

"I do."

"Why?"

Now I was embarrassed.

"Because I haven't had sex in five years."

"You're shitting me."

"No. I'm not."

"Nobody goes that long without sex."

"I do—or I did."

"Shit."

"Yeah!"

We both laughed. He looked at me closely.

"Why me?"

After the laughter, I had hoped the conversation would become easier. Instead, it was getting harder.

"Because I liked watching you out the window."

"There are a lot of guys out the window—your next-door neighbor."

"No. Not him."

I still hadn't answered his question so he asked it again.

"Why me?"

He wanted a reason and deserved it.

"Because when I watched you sawing, I watched how you held the wood and I wanted you to hold me like you held the wood."

I was close to tears and didn't want to be. I didn't think "being so needy you are close to tears" would win over a potential bedmate. Everything was in pieces. My black leather skirt and little black heels were irrelevant. I was sitting in a room with a man, a girlfriend, and a daughter. He was sitting with a woman who wanted to trade places with a 2×4.

Trent took another long haul on his beer and finally spoke. "So with the sex, what are we talking?"

"What do you mean?"

"Are we talking once or more than once?"

Oh! I hadn't even considered more than once. Fireworks of possibility went off in my head.

"How about once but if we like it, we could do it more

than once—if we both like it."

He looked out the window and then back. "Sounds like a plan."

I just looked at him. I was going to have sex! With this man! I said nothing. I couldn't. The fireworks were too loud.

"So, when do you want to do it?"

"When?"

"Yeah. When do you want to have sex?"

"Oh! I don't know."

In my mental imaginings of this conversation, I had never gotten this far, to the decision and then the practicalities of scheduling. Trent was way ahead of me.

"How about Sunday?"

"This Sunday?"

"Yeah. This Sunday. That would be the day after tomorrow."

He was smiling. I smiled and laughed. We agreed on five o'clock on Sunday afternoon.

I had both of my hands on the table because I had been using them to hold myself upright. He drained his beer and put the unopened second can back in his pocket. We both started to stand but then he covered my right hand with his left and kissed me. I fell back into my chair as the kiss continued. His mouth was warm and beery. Not only had I not had sex in five years, but I hadn't been kissed in five years. This felt very, very good.

We stood and kissed some more. As we broke apart he looked down at my black tights and said, "Don't wear those on Sunday."

I closed the door behind him and stood on the porch. We had really been here, we had really had this conversation, and he had really kissed me! I picked up his empty beer can and put my mouth where his mouth had been. I thought about Sunday.

Saturday, October 4, 2003

I waited.

I thought about what I would wear. I decided on a chamois-colored skirt that looked and felt like suede—I thought he would like the feel of it—and a tight V-neck print top that went with it. It was one of those outfits I'd bought when I started dating men from the dating service. I'd never worn it.

The dating service men were mortgage brokers, bankers, lawyers, and one of them was retired. They were all nice enough but I didn't connect with any of them. I had dated a handful when I realized I was connecting better with the men I was working with than the men I was dating. The men I worked with were commercial-property building engineers and construction managers. They lived in the physical world, the world of machines and tools and blueprints and physics. They could fix things. They told stories about their wives and kids. They referred to their buildings as "she" and took good care of them.

I had called the dating service and asked if they had any "just guys."

"Just guys?"

"Yeah—guys whose job it is to build things or fix things. Just guy guys."

The dating service man didn't respond. I figured out the reason and offered it. "Guys like that don't use a dating service, do they?"

"No. They don't."

I thanked him and asked him to cancel the remainder of my twelve-man subscription.

Saturday night I lay in bed in the guest bedroom and thought about what I was about to do. In high school I had decided that I would never be one of those girls who dated her friend's boyfriend. Now I was about to sleep with a friend's boyfriend, a boyfriend she had been with for five years.

Jane had told me she wasn't interested in him. I could take her at her word. If she had deceived me, then I could deceive her. While my head was busy looking for justification, my body let me know I wanted to have sex with Trent. I put my head aside. Let the chips fall.

I did not sleep that night for a long time. I lay on my back with my hands at my sides and felt the pull below my belly that wanted him. I knew I was swollen. I could feel the river.

Sunday, October 5, 2003

I took a shower and shaved my legs. The chamois skirt and the knit top were laid out on the bed. I put them on. In a bathroom drawer I found some mascara and a lipstick. I didn't know what else to do so I sat on the living room couch, smoothed my skirt beneath me, and waited. I looked at my watch. It was a little after three thirty. I got a book but couldn't read, so I got a different book with lots of pictures and looked.

At five o'clock, the doorbell rang.

I met him at the front door. We hadn't been at the front of the house since the first day, when he had come to do the estimate. He was wearing a nice light-yellow sweatshirt, not the camouflage one he had been wearing when we arranged this meeting, and clean jeans, not dusty shorts. We were seeing each other in clothes we had never seen each other in before. He looked down and noted my stockings. I thought I saw a whiff of disappointment cross his face.

I led the way up the stairs and hoped he liked my skirt. In the living room, I noticed that he had a six-pack in each hand—Icehouse for him and Rolling Rock for me. I thought it considerate that he had thought about what beer I might like. We walked back to the kitchen and each took a beer. When I came back after putting the rest of the beers in the fridge, he had opened my beer for me and I thought that was nice, too. I took a sip and thought what I think every time I taste beer: *It tastes like my father.*

We went back to the living room and sat on the couch. I took another sip of the beer, to be polite. I drink wine, not beer.

I was deciding what to talk about when he kissed me. His lips felt like they had before. They still felt good. He didn't stop kissing and neither did I. His hand was on my leg and the small part of my brain that could still think concluded that the chamois skirt had been an excellent choice. Then I felt the heat of his hand on my thigh and realized that his hand was no longer on top of my skirt, but under my skirt and heading north. When the tips of his long fingers reached the top of my stocking, his hand suddenly stopped. Then it moved sideways and found the rubber and metal clip of my garter. My lips could feel his curve up in a smile.

We headed to the bedroom and I was surprised at how quickly his clothes were gone. Maybe he had already started taking them off on the way to the bedroom. There was a naked (gloriously naked!) man standing in my bedroom, his jeans and briefs at his ankles, stopped from further progress by his work boots. I was fully clothed. I hurried to catch up as he pulled at his boots.

We jumped into bed and landed on our knees. The first thing he did was lick the outside of my thigh, once, a friendly greeting, like a golden retriever might, a physical, "Hey, let's have fun!" I laughed and then thought that maybe I shouldn't be laughing during hot sex, and with that thought covered my mouth with my hand.

"I think laughter is good," he said.

"Really?"

"Yeah. It kind of . . . greases the wheels."

And then he made me laugh some more.

During sex, when we were sideways on the bed, I said something that was the kind of thing the man I had been married to, the man who had caught my eye with his purple suspenders, liked to hear during sex. By the constriction in Trent's eyes, I could tell he suddenly knew more about me than he wanted to know. I was embarrassed and turned my head away. But only for a moment.

Afterward, Trent held me. We were nested, folded together, his arms curled around mine. I was glad he couldn't see my face because my eyes were wet. He had just showed me what sex was supposed to be like. He knew how many years it had been since I last had sex but he didn't know how many men I'd slept with. He was the second.

So much care, so much attention and thoughtfulness had come from his body into mine. Tears for all I had not been given went sideways out of my eyes and down into my pillow. I would have sobbed if he had not been there. I told myself to be still, to be grateful for the man wrapping himself around me, now falling asleep. I looked at his arm, with its flock of curling blond hairs, and beneath them, the tanned skin, and beneath that, the cords of his forearm. I looked at his hand, at the long strong fingers and the wide thumb, set low on his palm. I looked at how gently, still, his fingers touched me, and I fell asleep.

3. Birth Control

October 6, 2003

I went to work the next morning and when I came home saw a note on the kitchen counter, written in all caps:

> Jule,
>
> Thank you for having me over last night. I had a very nice time. Get some rest and I will see you soon. Take care!
>
> Your special friend Trent
>
> P.S. Making love to you is great! (just like Tony the Tiger would say it)

He was the one who brought it up.

"What are we going to do about birth control?"

I made an appointment with my doctor. He could see me quickly, which was a relief. "For how long do you wish to preserve your fertility?" he asked. I told him that at forty-six I was too old to have a baby, even if all the equipment seemed to be working. He wrote out a prescription for the patch and we scheduled an appointment to make getting pregnant impossible.

October 20, 2003

I passed the prescription across the pharmacy counter and left with my brand-new box of contraceptive patches.

On Tuesday morning, after my shower, I took one out of the box, peeled it from its wrapper, and put it on my skin, just inside my right hip bone. I liked the little square patch with the rounded corners. It made me feel sexy. I was having sex!

For some reason, that same morning Trent drove to Michigan and then drove back to Chicago to see me. When I saw him that night, we started out on the living room floor but I couldn't stay there. I was sick.

I pulled myself up from the floor and went to the bedroom, fell onto the bed with my head at the foot of the bed, and pulled my knees to my chest. My belly was knotted in pains that made me push my legs out and then pull them back in again.

I am naked and I am embarrassed and I am too sick to stand up. Trent appears in the doorway. He looks upside down because I have curled my head back to see him. He is naked and I want him to go away. I don't know what is wrong with me and I hurt. He doesn't go away. He comes and sits beside me. He cups his hand on my head and feels my forehead. I can see in his eyes that he is not angry or disgusted or even disappointed. He is worried. He asks if I have a robe he can get for me. He is a naked man who doesn't even know me well enough to know if I have a robe, and he is getting it for me.

After some time of lying in the robe, curled up on the bed with my head in his lap and telling him, "No, I don't want to go to the emergency room," I decided that the cause of the pain was the little flesh-colored square that didn't match the flesh it was sticking to. The contractions that were pulling at my belly and my legs were familiar. They were stronger, painfully stronger, but I knew the source. I went to the bathroom and pulled off the patch. I went back to bed. I don't remember what Trent did.

I woke up exhausted and still nauseous but at least the contractions that had folded me in half had stopped. In the bathroom, I took the stuck-together patch that was lying in a little puddle of water on the sink and threw it into the trash. I went to work and came home. Trent had been waiting for me. We tried to fit ourselves together the way we wanted to but couldn't. My body wanted to be alone. My body wanted to rest.

We made love the following night and the morning after that but not the next night because Trent had left. He had left and gone to Jane's.

Late October 2003

We were lying on our backs in bed in the Chicago house, trying to get to know each other better and asking each other questions. I asked him about growing up.

"How many vehicles have you owned?" he asked me.

"Five. Why? What about you?"

Trent worked through the fingers on his left hand, then his right, then back to his left. Then he wiggled a couple of fingers on his right hand.

"About twenty."

"So many?"

"I crashed a few."

"So you don't know exactly how many cars you've had?"

"Sometimes it's hard to know how to count."

"What do you mean?"

"If I crashed a car that I was going to buy but hadn't bought yet, should I count it?"

When Trent was seventeen, he had taken his uncle Bernie's Land Cruiser—which he called a Land Cruncher—out on the road, one of the few times he drove the speed limit. He had just come over the crest of a hill to find a car stopped right in front of him. He swerved around it and then back to avoid an oncoming car, rolling over and ending up in a field. The car was totaled. His plan had been to walk back to his uncle's house, but a state police officer pulled up and stopped him.

"You need to go to the hospital, son."

"I do not."

"Your lip's bleeding."

"I happen to know they won't stitch that up."

"Maybe not, but your shoulder's dislocated."

"Is not."

"Take a look."

The police officer reached down, picked up the broken-off side mirror, and held it up so Trent could see himself. Trent saw his left shoulder hanging down about mid-chest level. The next day, lying in the hospital bed, a different police officer came to the doorway.

"Are you Trent Price?"

Trent thought about lying but decided it would be pretty hard to pull off, given the situation. He steeled himself for whatever the officer had to say next.

"Son, you're a hell of a driver."

The officer explained that he had set up cones where the stopped car had been, then driven his car down the road at the speed Trent had been going, then swerved to avoid the cones. He tried three times, and, even knowing that the cones were there, was never able to avoid hitting them.

"I'm a good driver, Sweet Baby. I can climb trees."

Trent's shoulder healed, but a large, bony knot formed on the top of his left shoulder, like a walnut slipped under the skin. He didn't like it. I loved everything about it. It was my rosary, my proof that Trent could survive anything.

Early November 2003

The medical profession refers to all invasive actions it performs on the human body as a procedure. It doesn't matter whether the loss is small—a wart—or massive—a lung. All actions are described under the generic, protective, and sometimes misleading term "procedure."

Mine was scheduled for a Monday and I was looking forward to it. The human body is fascinating and medical advances intrigue me. I had been happy to learn that, as with many other procedures, scalpels were used less and less, even for this procedure.

The Friday before the procedure, a nurse called to make sure I knew when to stop eating and when to stop drinking. She also told me that I needed to have someone drive me; I absolutely could not drive myself home. This was not a reminder; this was news—and it was a problem.

The hospital was in Downers Grove, a western suburb, twenty-six miles from my Lincoln Square two-flat on the northern side of Chicago. Trent was in Michigan. My good friends were all in the suburbs. I called Trent. He said he needed to stay in Michigan. I hung up unhappy and angry. Why was I doing this for a man who wouldn't even drive me? Was I once again giving myself over to a man who would treat me poorly? Should I go through with it? I was being irrational and I knew it. I wasn't doing this for Trent—I was doing it for me.

I ended up calling the only friend I had in the city, David.* He had moved there about the same time I did. I drove us to the hospital and David drove us back. When I got home I went to bed and cried for the babies I always thought I would have but never did and never would.

The next morning I went to Boston. On the plane and all through the seven days I was in Boston and Providence, I thought about Trent.

When I came back, a vase of flowers stood outside my door. Trent had asked earlier whether I liked roses. I had told him that I liked roses but not red ones because they remind me of funerals. The vase held no red roses.

4. A Calendar

November 2003

Halfway through October I had started keeping a calendar because I was so surprised at what was happening that I wanted something to help me remember, if it ended, that it had really happened. I recorded everything important that happened with Trent and some things that weren't. Sometimes I added locations.

It tells me that on the morning after our first night I caught a flight to Dallas for work. I have no memory of the trip. It tells me that Trent and I managed to get together throughout October, that we had sex often, and that toward the end of the month I got sick.

I wrote in two colors. The blue notations were the dates I got to be with Trent. The black notations began in late November, added when I realized that the times Trent wasn't with me he was with Jane.

When we had talked that first Friday evening and he had proposed Sunday night for our sex date, he had not proposed Saturday because he knew he would be with her. He was with her until he told her he went back to Michigan, except that he came to my house instead.

I recorded the days that he was most likely with her because I wanted to be honest about this relationship. I was in a triangle.

I told myself that I knew what I was getting into the first time I slept with him. I told myself that I was the one who put three people in this relationship. I told myself whatever I told myself because it felt so good to be in Trent's arms that I would do anything to feel his arms around me, to lie next to him with our elbows and our calves and the sides of our feet touching, to slide my hand into the warm fur of his chest, to sleep with my hand resting cradled by his.

The bed we slept in was the one I had gotten after my divorce, when I walked away from the man in the purple suspenders and the black bed with dark-purple sheets. I had spotted this bed in an antique store near my apartment, the tall golden oak headboard and slightly lower footboard leaning against a wall. I saw no price. The owner responded curtly.

"It's not for sale yet."

Several months later, the bed was mine. Before he rang up the sale, though, the owner pointed out the carefully crafted split grain and warned me to never move the bed by dragging it on a carpet. The bed must be lifted.

A loud *crack* one night moved us to the guest bedroom. The next morning when I came home from work, Trent had an update.

"I checked the bed. It can be glued back together."

He drank some of his beer, adding, "I can glue it, but I'm not a finish carpenter. I can put it back together but it might not be perfect."

"I'd rather you put it back together than someone else."

He nodded. "I'm going to need four six-foot C-clamps to do it."

"Okay."

"They cost about thirty bucks a piece."

Now I understood. Trent was asking me for $120 to buy C-clamps.

Until then I had thought that Trent was a successful general contractor. I knew he "rehabbed houses in Chicago" but that was all. Now I knew he didn't have a spare $120 to buy tools.

I came home one evening and Trent was sitting on the kitchen floor, which was strange. He looked strange. He wasn't supposed to be at my house, he was supposed to be at Jane's. I said that she was expecting him and he should go.

"Just because it doesn't bother you doesn't mean it doesn't bother me," he said angrily.

"I never said it doesn't bother me. It bothers me every time I watch your back go out that door. But I know what I signed up for."

Not too long after that, Jane called me to plan a breakfast together, one of those things that we always said we were going to do but never did. We went to a small and noisy restaurant, packed because they have thick bacon and real corn bread. Neither of us mentioned Trent but we both knew he was the only reason we were sitting across from each other at a tiny table in a pink room eating food but not tasting it.

I wanted to hurt Jane for lying to me about Trent. I lied to her then and we both knew that I was lying.

"It sure would be nice to go out on a date."

Jane didn't react, so I pushed it. I wanted to put the knife in and twist it.

"I really miss having sex."

Then I asked the server if I could buy my coffee mug. I wanted a souvenir.

One night, on the heels of Trent going out the back door

to go to Jane's, I took my breakfast-with-Jane-souvenir-coffee-mug out of the cupboard. I wanted to smash it. I swung my arm back above my head and threw the mug to the floor as hard as I could throw it. It hit the yellow maple floor, bounced up, and hit the wall. It fell back down and rolled across the floor, leaving a mug-sized hole in the wall. It was undamaged. Not even a chip. I picked it up and threw it in the garbage.

Later, Trent and I were holding each other, standing in the kitchen. He looked down at the hole in the wall.

"What happened?"

"A coffee mug hit it."

He looked at me. "How?"

"I threw it."

"You threw a mug at the wall?"

"No, I threw a mug at the floor and it bounced up and hit the wall."

"Why?"

"I threw it when you went to Jane's. I wanted to break it. But it didn't break."

"Pretty tough mug."

We both laughed.

The next day I came home from work and there was a white circle of fresh spackling on the wall, filling and concealing the hole. I looked at Trent.

"What happened?"

"I figured since I was part of causing it, I might as well be part of fixing it."

November 2003

"I love you."

It came out, unexpected and unwanted, during sex. Trent said it and we both looked away.

The next morning he was gone. He left a note behind, a small square green Post-it. I know what the note said because I still have it. It is in the blue wooden box with all the notes he left me that I saved, and all the notes I left him that he saved. He wrote in all capital letters:

> Jule,
>
> I shouldn't have said that word that starts with an
>
> L and ends with an E but that's just the way I feel.
>
> Trent

That night I called him and asked him to come over. We stood in the kitchen and held each other. We said nothing for a while. We held each other and looked at each other with this fresh knowing floating between us. Then I spoke.

"Are we going to be all right?"

"As long as we keep loving each other and telling each other the truth, we're going to be fine."

I thought about that, weighing both halves of Trent's equation. I tested it by talking it through.

"The truth is important."

"It is. If you don't have the truth, you don't have anything. It's all pretend."

"Love is important, too."

"Baby, love is stronger than anything. Even titanium."

5. Scars

November 2003

Somehow, in the thrill of having a naked man in my bedroom, I had failed to notice the scars on his body.

This time when he walked into the bedroom, I didn't meet his eyes. I looked instead at the large, shiny marks crisscrossing the lower part of his torso. There had to be more than ten, maybe twenty of them. The largest ones were an inch or more wide and ran the full width of his abdomen. The smaller ones were maybe two-thirds as long and not quite as wide. There was one very short one—maybe only three inches—in the middle. They were set at various angles, as if he had lain down and someone above had dropped pick-up sticks on his belly that had turned flesh-colored, melted, and hardened in a bizarre metamorphosis. All the scars were blunt at one end and pointed at the other. He saw me looking and said nothing. He lifted the covers, moved in beside me, and made me forget the scars.

A few nights later, as he sat on the bed and I sat beside him, I looked more closely. We were silent until I spoke.

"Those aren't from a machine."

He said nothing. I wanted to know how those scars got there. I was trying to imagine what kind of circumstance would make those marks. I spoke again.

"They're not from an accident."

I waited but still he said nothing. I ventured out farther onto the thin ice of the shiny, wrinkled flesh.

"Someone did this."

At this Trent tilted his head back, took in and let out a long breath, then brought his head back to level before he spoke.

"Yes."

I didn't know what else to say and he said no more, so I tilted him back, laid him down on the bed, and began to kiss the scars. I was determined to kiss each one for its entire length. It took a long time. I got confused at the middle where there was so much crisscrossing that I lost my way. Before I could finish, Trent rolled me over and started kissing me. We made love, slowly, looking each other in the eye, never looking away.

We slept until something hurt me. It was Trent and he was kicking. Me. Hard. He was facing away from me and his heels were slamming into my shins on the recoil, his legs flailing off the bed in the full forward extension. I yelled and that woke him. He stopped kicking and turned to face me.

"Why did you yell?"

"Because you were kicking me."

"I'm sorry."

"Why were you kicking?"

"A bad dream."

"About what?"

"I was at Ralston's and I couldn't get out."

"What's Ralston's?"

"Where I used to work."

These dreams and this kicking happened many, many times. I learned that Trent had gone to Ralston Foods when he graduated from high school (more accurately, was graduated so the school could be done with him). He worked in the factory, doing shift work. Ralston would call him in or tell him to stay home on a schedule that seemed nothing more than a whim. He would work a night shift and go home and try to sleep. Ralston would get him out of bed and tell him to come back in. He would be told to hold a weekend for work and then never get called in. He knew that if he ever balked there were many more men and women who would readily step in and take his place and his paycheck.

Trent started out eager in his work but after two days the more senior guys told him to slow down, or else. He didn't slow down so the guys backed him against a wall and told him again. This time he understood and obeyed. He began to sleep under the scale during the night shift and during the day shift when he had worked the previous night. He opened forty-pound boxes of raisins with his elbows and dumped them into a huge vat of cereal, for ten hours at a time. He told me that when Sam's Club wanted extra raisins in their raisin bran and Ralston did it, the cereal boxes broke apart from the added weight and moisture. When the workers struck, Trent struck with them. When the strike ended, it was Trent's photo on the cover of the Battle Creek newspaper, taking down the plywood "STRIKE!" sign from the chain-link fence. When Trent went back to work, he was laid off. He'd worked at Ralston for fifteen years.

At first I thought the nightmares and the kicking were about Ralston, but I realized later that they were really about Trent's father. It was his father who had worked at and retired from Ralston and it was his father who had encouraged Trent to "get a good factory job." That, though, wasn't why Trent kicked.

I don't know when the beatings started. I do know they didn't stop until the last one, when Trent was seventeen.

In a small, square photograph, Trent and his sister stand in front of a Christmas tree. The outside border is still white but the inside colors have been washed with yellow. Judging by Trent's size and his sister's unsteadiness on her feet, I'm guessing Trent is about four years old. I had wondered what he looked like as a little boy. This photo, instead of giving me pleasure, made me sad. *It's already started*, I thought. *He's already been hurt.* You could see it in his eyes and the way he stood, pushing out his chest, trying to make himself look bigger than he really was.

When Trent was maybe eight or nine, he began intervening when his father beat his mother, Jean. Trent was successful in his distraction and replacement, substituting his body for hers.

When he was older, his father—Herb—went after Trent directly. Trent was big and at fifteen or sixteen was already bigger than his father. But Trent never hit his father back. Instead, he offered up himself as a living punching bag. His father was careful to never hit Trent's face. Until the last time.

The last time, his father first choked him and then hit him in the face. Something about being struck in the face broke something or brought something to life in Trent. He hit back. Both father and son wound up bloody. The father went to the emergency room. Trent did not. He ran instead to his girlfriend's house but her parents saw the blood and wouldn't let him in. He never said where he stayed that night.

When he went home the next day, his mother met him at the door. He thought she would say she was sorry. Instead, she told him that sons aren't supposed to hit their fathers and that he couldn't live there any longer. She closed the door.

I believed him when he told me these things because of the details. He described how, when his father had his hands around Trent's neck, Trent could see his father's tongue between his square teeth, the teeth pressing into his tongue, with blood coming out of the indentations where his teeth were pressing.

Trent cried when he told me this. He pounded his arms down on the mattress and said, "I shouldn't have hit him. I should have let him beat me." I screamed, "No!" and cried, too. I threw my leg over him and wrapped my arms around him and held him as tightly as I could and I said, "No, no, no, no, no. Please. No."

I came home from work and Trent was not there, which was a surprise. He had left me a letter. I took it to the living room and sat down on the couch. Whatever it said, I wanted to be sitting.

It was long, three pages of blue-lined white paper, each covered in Trent's block print. The first page was neat but the handwriting got sloppier as it went on. The paper was wrinkled, especially the last page, but the themes were clear.

I am a drunk.

I am $17,000 in debt.

I have a bad temper.

I love you and I should go away.

I read it, read it again, and then once more. I was surprised that I wasn't surprised and that it didn't make me want to tell him to go away. I feared I might be reverting to the woman I had been when I was married to the man in the purple suspenders. I called my friend Elaine, who is also my therapist, and asked how quickly I could see her.

I loved this man but I would not if it meant that loving him was not loving myself. I couldn't go back there. I couldn't go back to that gray place where I cried every day and didn't even know why I was crying.

6. Therapy

1986, Graduate School, Minneapolis, Minnesota

To understand why my first reaction to getting Trent's letter was to call Elaine, I need to go backward and tell you about her. And to tell you about her, I need to go further back and tell you about my history with therapy.

"If you haven't been through therapy, you should. Every one of you. If you intend to do this work, you need to work through your own stuff first."

The man speaking was Dr. Gary McLean, professor of organizational development at the University of Minnesota and my major professor. He had a slow physical manner that belied a quick mind. He would pause, appear to be finished with that portion of the lecture, and walk back to his notes. Then he would stop, turn, and ask a question that quieted the room. He was an academic Columbo.

His office was at the end of a long narrow hall and filled with papers and books. He was in a newer portion of the building that had been recently attached, so instead of thick limestone walls and small windows, he had a large window behind his desk trimmed with a narrow band of metal. The stacks of papers and books seemed to be his attempt at thickening the walls. He beckoned me to come in.

I didn't sit. I stood and blurted my question. "What therapist should I see?"

"What?"

"In class, you said that if we want to work in organizational development then we should make sure we have our own heads on straight. I have never seen a therapist so I need to know which one I should see."

"Ah, yes. Excellent."

"Do you know any?"

"Yes, I do."

He paused to look at me and think. I imagined photos of various therapists flashing next to me in his mind. He picked one.

"Mary Ursu. See Mary."

Ever the obedient student, I called Mary Ursu and scheduled my appointment. Her office was in a stretch of Minneapolis that had once been residential, with neat rows of brick four-squares built in the 1920s. The city had breathed in, grown larger, and her block was now a light business district. The occupants of each house—dentists and lawyers and chiropractors—were described by their neatly lettered wood signs in their well-kept front lawns. I walked up the cement steps.

At the end of my obligatory session, I prepared to close both the conversation and my relationship with Mary Ursu.

"So, we're done."

"Yes, for today."

"Oh. Am I supposed to come back?"

"I think that would be good."

I assumed the return appointment would be at a dentist's or a doctor's interval—six months for a dentist, twelve months for a doctor.

"When should I come back?"

"Can you come next week?"

"Next week?"

"Yes. Can you come next week?"

"So we're not done?"

"I think we have some more to talk about."

"What will we talk about?"

"I think we'll start with your father and then we'll talk about your mother."

"But why would we talk about them?"

And then Mary repeated two sentences that had seemed rational when I spoke them during my appointment but sounded totally absurd coming out of her mouth. I saw her weekly for several months until graduation. Every session ended with me walking down her concrete steps with a crushing headache. I learned to pack aspirin for the trip. Moments of our conversation I still remember decades later. One of her questions was, "What similarities do you see between your family growing up and the church you are in now?"

Mary Ursu was a smart woman and a good therapist. When I first came to the University of Minnesota, I felt lost. So I went to the New Student Activities Fair and signed up for two student groups—an outdoor adventuring group and a religious group. The people in the outdoor group never called me but the people in the religious group did. They were friendly and seemed quite nice. The group may have been a cult.

I say "may have been a cult." You can decide. The church had certain rules: expected service six days a week, required all members to live together, kept track of each member's tithing, forbade dating, and required approval from the elders for marriage. Its members shunned me when I left.

Even now I can feel what that felt like, to travel back for a wedding and have people turn from me, to sit in a long pew in a crowded church and have only one person, a former roommate who was also shunned, share the pew with me.

I was in that church for ten years, starting when I transferred to the university and ending when I escaped to a new job in Illinois, which I got by going back to school to get my master's degree. Dr. McLean was my adviser, which is what led me to see a therapist. Mary Ursu helped me see that I had picked a church that mirrored my family.

1988, Internship, St. Charles, Illinois

A few weeks after leaving the church for my job in Illinois, I met a man at work who was wearing a purple tie and purple suspenders. He was fascinating and charming and entertaining. He asked me out, and after six dates I had sex with him because I had spent the last ten years in a church where you couldn't have sex with a man unless you were married to him. I had obeyed the rules and I was about to turn thirty-one and I didn't want to obey the rules anymore.

1993, Marriage, Naperville, Illinois

After we had lived together for two years and been married for three, he said I didn't seem happy. He said there was something wrong with me. He said I should see a therapist and get some medication.

The counselor's name was Carole. I liked Mary better—Mary's style was more comforting and compassionate and she had a Ph.D. But Carole was covered by employee health insurance so I saw her instead.

After a few sessions, Carole said, "Don't you find it interesting that your family, your former church, and your marriage are all essentially the same?"

Her question had implications I wasn't ready to deal with. After one more session, so that I could pretend that her question wasn't the reason, I stopped seeing her.

1997

Four years later, I couldn't breathe. Literally. My asthma started when the man in the purple suspenders and I got the cats that I agreed to get because I grew tired of protesting that I am allergic to cats. I had read that after a period of time the body should adjust to cats and the symptoms should ease, but my asthma got worse. I had inhalers everywhere—the nightstand, kitchen drawer, glove compartment, briefcase. It didn't matter how many inhalers I had and how often I used them. I was gasping for air.

I switched doctors and my new internist was appalled at my answer to how frequently I was using a rescue inhaler: about twenty times a day. He wrote a prescription for a corticosteroid, saying that it would make me less dependent on the rescue inhaler.

My mother is a sensible woman, eminently practical. Once, in college when I got sick, I complained to her, "My body is betraying me." Her response was simple: "You're betraying your body." She taught me that my body will always tell me what it needs, if I listen.

I needed to find out what my body was trying to tell me. A work colleague gave me the name of her naprapath, an alternative medicine practitioner. The naprapath asked me more questions during her exam than I had been asked in my previous ten years of annual physical exams with regular doctors. She asked about bodily functions and excretions, diet and disease, sleeping and waking. For the first half hour, I answered her questions. For the second half hour, I cried as I answered her questions. She made notes and I waited to hear her diagnosis.

"Basically, you're healthier than most people I see, but something is making you very sad and you need to find out what that is."

"Oh."

And then I cried some more.

Later, my friend Rose said, "Elaine is wonderful. Call Elaine." Rose was my best source for the name of a therapist, a good one, who could help me figure out what was making me so sad. On my second visit, I sat on the edge of Elaine's green couch, my feet firmly on the carpet, my arms lifted above me for emphasis.

"But I am happy!"

The tears were streaming down my face. And the little voice inside my head, the one I hadn't listened to for so long, said, *You've just lied to a therapist.* And what was worse was that I realized I was also lying to myself. I walked down the wooden steps from Elaine's second-floor office and left my pretense behind. I took an inventory of my life.

"I have a good job, I live in a nice house, and I am not happy." I was surprised.

For my third visit to Elaine, I crafted a question. If I didn't like her answer, I wouldn't be back.

Sitting forward on her couch, I asked, "What is your philosophy of therapy?"

"You know, I was just thinking about that recently."

"So how would you describe it?"

"To create a safe place for the client—"

Her arms, in their soft lime-green sweater and sparkly bracelet, went out and made a large circle.

"A place," she continued, "where all of the client is heard and honored—the clean parts, the dirty parts, the angry parts, the nice parts, the afraid parts . . . I want to create a safe space where the whole of the individual is respected and honored."

Her answer was more than enough. It was perfect.

September 1997

On my fourth visit, I waited anxiously for the previous client to wrap up so I could tell Elaine my news.

"I left him on Saturday."

"Your husband?"

"Uh-huh."

"What happened?"

"I wanted to go on a bicycle ride and he forbade me."

"He forbade you?"

"That's what I said to him. 'Since when do we forbid each other to do something? I don't forbid you from going to strip clubs and all I want to do is go on a bicycle ride.' He didn't want me to go."

"What kind of bicycle ride was it? One of those three-day things or . . . ?"

"No. It was just a ride along Lake Michigan with friends—Anne* and Denise and Jane. I was going to take Friday afternoon off for the ride, stay over at Jane's on Friday night, and come back Saturday. It was just a bicycle ride. What kind of marriage is it where you can't even go on a bicycle ride?"

"What happened?"

"We fought about it all week. Every night I would come home from work, he would bring it up and we would fight about it again. One night we were up until one in the morning."

"Why didn't you just tell him you were going on the ride and then go to bed, rather than stay up until one in the morning fighting?"

"Oh. I guess I didn't think about that as a possibility."

"Did you end up going or not?"

"Oh, I went!"

"Wonderful. And how was it?"

"It was great. The weather was perfect, the lake was gorgeous—we had a great time."

"So you didn't spend the bike ride thinking about him?"

"No. I called him right before I left work but he still didn't want me to go. I didn't think about him again until after the ride, at dinner. They all knew he didn't want me to go and asked if I wanted to call him now that we were back. It was so nice to be out on the patio, having a good meal and laughing with friends. I said no, I didn't want to call him, I didn't feel like it."

"So you go on the ride, you have dinner, you have a great time, then what?"

"I stayed over at Jane's and then the next morning, instead of going home, I went to work."

"You didn't want to go home?"

"No, he would just yell at me. Besides, we had a big deadline at work. My part was done but one of my colleagues had a nervous breakdown and we all had to divvy up her part and get it done for Tuesday."

"So it's Saturday and you're at work. Then what?"

"About eleven in the morning, I called him because I felt bad about us fighting. We started fighting again and then he told me something and I knew I was never going home again."

The words tumbled out of me.

"When we started fighting again I thought, *Forget it, I can't talk to this guy*, and I told him I was going to hang up. Just as I'm starting to put the phone down I can hear him say, 'Wait! I have something to tell you. It's important.' I said, 'What?' And he said, 'Your Aunt Olga died.' And I said, 'When did she die?' And he said, 'Thursday.' I said, 'When did you find out?' And he said, 'Thursday, before you came home from work.' I said, 'Why didn't you tell me on Thursday?' And he said, 'Because I want us to focus on what is most important and our marriage is most important.' And I said, 'You didn't tell me when you saw me on Thursday, you didn't tell me when we talked on Friday, and the only reason you're telling me now is to keep me from hanging up. I have to go now.' I hung up the phone and I just sat there staring at it, wondering what kind of man was on the other end. I knew then I was never going home again."

"What did you do?"

"I left work and went to a hotel close by. I'm still there but I need to leave because it's getting too expensive."

"Where can you go?"

"I suppose I could call Anne and see if I can stay with her and Dean.* I know other people have done that when they've been in trouble." I slumped into the couch and said softly, "I lied to him. I told him I'm still working on the project but I'm not. I haven't told him I'm not coming back."

Elaine paused before asking her next question. "Do you want to try couples therapy?"

The air came out of my lungs as I imagined sitting next to him on Elaine's couch. I barely had enough air to speak.

"No. I don't. When I think about it, it feels like trying to push a boulder up a huge mountain. It feels too big."

By this point I was slumped forward, chest caved down toward my lap, barely able to hold myself up. I wanted to lie down. Instead, I put my fist under my chin to hold my head up. I just sat there. I wasn't even crying. I was too tired.

Elaine spoke. "What do you want to do?"

"I suppose I should tell him. I should tell him I'm leaving."

"How do you think that will go?"

"Badly. If he didn't even want me to go on a bicycle ride. . ." I slumped further. Not even my arm could hold me up.

Elaine spoke again. "Normally I don't say things like this to clients, but I'm concerned for your safety. Based on what you have told me about him, I believe that you're right, that he won't take the news well. I'm concerned that he may retaliate and hurt you."

"What should I do?"

"First, do you think you can stay with Anne and Dean?"

"Yeah. They have fighting couples—I mean, half of the couple—stay with them all the time."

"Can you call him from their house?"

"I don't want to talk to him. I want to write it down. Then I don't have to talk to him."

At work, I composed the letter. At lunch, I went home and put the letter on the kitchen counter. The next day over lunch, I went back again to grab some work clothes that I should have thought to take the day before. I saw a lawyer who advised me that if there was anything in the house I really wanted, I should go get it, saying, "Possession is nine-tenths of the law." Other than lunchtime reconnaissance missions to get more of my clothes, some important books, my jewelry, and my grandmother's quilt, I never went home again.

Elaine was right. He did retaliate, just not right away. A year later, after I moved out of my third-floor apartment and into my tiny Naperville house, he acted. He stalked me—methodically, consistently, and persistently. The police were involved, then a detective, then a private investigator. It lasted for half a year, until he made a mistake and then it stopped. I had heard him say frequently before I left him, "Revenge is a dish best served cold."

7. The Letter

November 2003

Sometimes, after leaving the man in the purple suspenders, I wondered. If I had been more steady on my feet after leaving Minnesota, if I hadn't been so freshly out of the church and recently ending therapy, if I had been stronger, if I had been more grounded and more sure of myself, would I have married him? And that is why, after I read Trent's three-page, tear-stained letter, I called Elaine.

I wanted Elaine to help me figure out whether Trent was a good man or another man in purple suspenders who would cage me and then frighten me. I thought Trent was a good man but I wanted a second opinion from a professional.

Elaine put on her half-glasses to read the letter. When she had finished, she took them off and looked at me.

"How long have you been seeing Trent?"

"A month—a little more."

"What do you think of what he wrote?"

"I don't know. There's so much there. I just . . . I feel like I should be scared but I'm not."

"You're not scared of any of it?"

"Well, the $17,000 is pretty frightening but . . . I don't know."

"So the debt scares you."

"It does. I mean, I grew up with 'debt is bad.' The only good debt is on an appreciating asset. $17,000 is a lot of money."

"It is. And it's not as much as some people owe."

"Really?"

"Really. There was a man here the other day who is $60,000 in debt. It's more common than you think."

"Oh."

"Does the drinking scare you?"

"No, and it probably should. But I grew up with that. That one I understand."

"Have you ever seen Trent drunk?"

"I think so. There was one night when I came home. He was sitting on the kitchen floor. I think he was drunk then."

"How was that?"

"It was sad. Not scary."

"What about the temper?"

"I've never seen it."

Elaine went silent. So I asked a question, hoping for an answer I wanted to hear: "What do you think?"

"I actually think this letter is good news. You've been seeing each other for roughly a month and he's just let you know everything he feels bad about, everything he's ashamed of."

She held the letter up. "This is from tears, yes?"

"I think so. And the handwriting just falls apart toward the end."

"He's ashamed of these things, he feels badly. He tells you about himself and then he asks you to tell him to go away."

"I think it's a cry for help."

"I do, too. Do you want to tell him to go away?"

"No. I don't. And I'm scared."

Elaine and I agreed that I would take things, as the AA people say, one day at a time. I would make sure that I felt safe and that I would let either Trent or Elaine know when I didn't. Elaine also offered to see Trent and me together if that was something I wanted.

As soon as I got home, I called him. He was close by, at the bar up the street, so got to my place quickly. We stood in the kitchen and held each other. I don't remember much talking. I do remember reminding him of his words, "As long as we keep loving each other and telling each other the truth, we're going to be okay."

I asked him, "How can you tell if someone loves you?" and waited through a long pause for his answer.

"By the way they hold you."

His arms were strong around me, firm, not crushing. His fingertips touched me lightly, as if he were trying to read me through my skin. His chest didn't feel hard or soft, it felt good. I wasn't contorting to fit myself to his form. It all felt good. He felt good.

About a year after Trent and I were established, I was at work and sitting in our weekly staff meeting. The icebreaker question that week was, "What is one of your favorite places in the world?" The answers were "Disneyland," "the islands of the Caribbean," "Napa Valley," and so on. My answer was, "In Trent's arms."

Meanwhile, the kicking was getting worse. We learned to sleep back-to-back so he wouldn't hurt me. It meant that we couldn't hold hands all night any more, but I felt safer. One morning the alarm went off and I looked over at Trent. He was already awake, flat on his back, eyes very wide. Something was wrong.

"What's wrong?"

"Nothing."

I looked at him, not harshly. I wanted him to know that I really wanted to know what was wrong. I wanted to know the truth, whatever the truth was. Maybe he decided I was ready to hear the truth. Maybe he just couldn't hold it in anymore.

"I want to kill myself."

"How do you want to do it?"

For some reason, I thought that if I knew the method I could take away the tool. If by hanging, take away the rope. If by sedation, take away the pills.

"With a gun."

I sighed and searched for an alternative,

"Well, will you at least promise not to kill yourself even if you feel like it?"

"That's what I'm doing."

One night as I was sitting up in bed, propped against pillows and reading, Trent looked at me and asked, "Sweet Baby, why do you like books so much?"

"It's like a book takes me to another place, someplace I didn't even know existed. It's like every book is a door to a whole new world to explore."

This is how I started reading to Trent at night, in bed, before we would fall asleep. For the first book, I wanted one he could relate to, something with a normal-seeming father who was really not normal. A dangerous father. A story with a happy ending, or as happy as it could be.

We started with *The Poisonwood Bible* by Barbara Kingsolver, a nice fat book that took a long time to get through. At the end, Trent wanted to know if it was a true story or not. Yes, it was based on true events but no, it was fiction. Next was *The Curious Incident of the Dog in the Night-*

Time, because I wanted a story about someone who overcame adversity. Trent wanted to know whether it was true.

"Sweet Baby, can we read a true story next time?"

This is how we came to *Endurance: Shackleton's Incredible Voyage,* the first book we read together that was new to both of us. It became Trent's favorite book.

November 2003

Trent came in through the back door carrying something in a big white bag. He didn't carry it by the handles of the bag; he carried it by the handle of whatever was in the bag. He handed it to me.

"What's this?"

"Open it."

The white bag had big black Crate & Barrel lettering on it. There was a substantial silver handle sticking out. The bag was crumpled around the handle where Trent had been holding it. I grabbed the handle with one hand and pulled the bag away with the other. It was a very large frying pan.

"Is this for me?"

"It's for here because I can't cook dippin' eggs in any of your pans."

A frying pan! Trent wanted to cook in my house!

"What are dippin' eggs?"

"Eggs over easy. It's what Jenna called them when she was little. I make them on Saturday mornings."

He wants to cook eggs here on Saturday mornings! He wants to be here on Saturdays! Not at Jane's.

I smiled and hugged him and who knows, we might have made love right there on the kitchen floor. All I remember is the frying pan and what I hoped it stood for.

Saturday came and Trent made dippin' eggs. They were good. Then he told me he needed to go to Jane's. He left and I washed the pan, wondering how long I could do this, wondering how long he could.

8. Mud Lake

November 2003

I had a headache. When I reached for the little white bottle of aspirin, the weight of it and the rattling sound told that it was almost empty. This was odd—I don't run out of aspirin because I hardly ever have headaches. I throw nearly full bottles away and replace them after a few years, when the expiration date has passed.

This bottle I'd bought only recently. Was Trent using up the aspirin? Why?

Trent was at Jane's. I comforted myself with the anticipation of going to his house the next weekend. He had invited me to spend it with him in Michigan. I would drive out Friday after work, stay there Friday night and Saturday, and drive back on Sunday.

He planned it for the weekend of November 21 through 23. The weekend after was no good because it was Thanksgiving and Trent would be spending it with Jenna. The weekend before was no good because it was the opening day of deer-hunting season. At the time, that meant nothing to me, but I now know that opening day of gun hunting is a holiday in Michigan. It's true—even schools are closed. Opening day is a holiday so that men (and some women) can put on warm clothes, sit outside for hours, come inside, drink beer, and eat whatever there is to eat. Sometimes they eat deer; most of the time they simply talk about the ones that got away.

At the time, I didn't know it: Trent didn't like to kill deer.

Trent would kill a deer but he hated it. He would kill a deer so that his cousins, who don't have much money or much food, had a decent meal to eat. What he liked was being outside and watching nature. He liked the smell of the air and waiting to see what he would see. He liked coming inside and getting warm, putting wood in the woodstove, and putting something to eat on top of the woodstove to cook. He liked turning up his music (classic rock) and telling stories that made people laugh.

After he died, I went through the box of deer-hunting photos that he kept high on a shelf in the garage that he called the lil' barn. Many are beautiful large black-and-whites, taken and developed by Trent's cousin Steven, who makes his living from his photography. A few were standard-sized color photos. One of these is proof that Trent liked the hunting but not the killing. Trent is holding up a dead deer by its antlers. There are a lot of points on the horns, and if I were a hunter I would have counted them. The horns are bloody and Trent's hands are bloody and he has blood on the front of his camouflage coat. His mouth is pulled to one side and his eyes are shiny and sad and he looks as if he's going to cry. I would lay money down that he got drunk that night, probably very drunk.

I didn't know these things, though, when I was anticipating that first visit. All I knew was that the house was on Mud Lake Road, well outside of Battle Creek. The house had a barn and stood on eighty acres. A creek ran through the property. Last, I needed to get off I-94 at exit 92 and then follow Trent's carefully written directions. I told myself that even if Trent was at Jane's, I was going to his house. I was the one he was bringing home.

November 21, 2003

My hands were tight on the wheel, tense in the snowstorm. My dog Charlie was asleep in the back seat. Trent's directions said to look for a white ranch with a chain-link fence around the front. Before I got that far, though, I had to pull over to the side of the road to brush the snow from a street sign so I could see whether that was the street I was supposed to turn left on or not. The snow was fluffy and sticky and I hadn't thought to put my gloves on before I got out of the car. My hands were red and wet on the steering wheel as I made the turn. The next right was easy and then it was just a matter of looking for a white house in a white snowstorm. I drove past it and then put the car in reverse.

Trent had left the wide front gate open for me. The house was a 1950s ranch with limestone on part of the front. Trent came out through the garage, not the front door, and that's the way I went in. He carried my bag as Charlie and I followed him past a blue bathroom and through a blue kitchen with pine cabinets and a floor of white tile with black grout. He put my bag down on the worn plywood floor of the dining room, from which the carpet had been pulled up long ago. Under the table was a brownish oriental-looking rug. The green carpet in the living room was discolored but intact. The dining room table was round with four captain's chairs around it. A large window looked out over the swamp, which stretched for a mile or more. Later I learned that sitting at that table and looking out over the swamp was the only part of the house that Trent liked.

Trent took us out to the barn—a long, low-slung red one with a finished front part and an unfinished back part that held canoes and so much other stuff that I couldn't tell what everything was. I could make out a large motor boat. Other than the canoes, most things looked like they had been in place for a long time, even the motor boat.

The pine-paneled front of the barn had an old woodstove, and Trent encouraged me to warm my hands by the fire. I held my hands to the little window, then realized the best place for heat was above the window, where the black metal was radiating the heat, and moved my hands there. I noticed a large stack of cut firewood against the wall that divided the finished part from the unfinished part and a massive workbench against the front wall. The end wall seemed to be taken up mostly with tools. The barn wasn't plain—it was decorated. Trent had hung things from the walls and the rafters—giant cross-sections from a cypress tree hung high on a wall and a colorful kite from the rafters. A large, bright-orange canvas sign courtesy of Budweiser proclaimed "Deer Hunters Welcome" below an aged wooden sign that read "C&C Ranchero." On the wall with the firewood was a large framed aerial map of the property. A boom box played from a shelf high on the wall of tools.

Trent, who had by this time learned that I don't drink beer, offered me a glass of wine. He had remembered the bottle but not a corkscrew so found a large screw and a pair of pliers and used those instead.

On Saturday morning, we went hunting on the creek that ran through the property, Trent in the bow of his wide brown canoe and me in the back, trying to paddle silently. It had stopped snowing but was cold enough that if the sky let loose again, it would be snow. Paddling silently was hard work, and sometimes I accidentally (and loudly) hit my hand on the cold, hard metal edge of the canoe. I thought, *He is testing me. This is a fucking test.* I wasn't sure whether I was angry or not. When we got back, Trent asked whether I'd seen the deer.

"What deer?" I asked.

He told me where the deer had been—a place where I remember the reeds moving. I asked him why he hadn't shot at it. "Killing a deer is a lot of work," he told me. "You have to haul it back, you have to hang it. I didn't want to take up the rest of our day with that."

On Saturday afternoon, I wanted to take a shower to get warm and clean but I didn't want to be naked in the shower/tub of the pink bathroom. A hole a few inches above the tub in the tile wall (A fist-sized hole? But too low to be from a punch?) had been covered by a piece of thick black garbage bag and duct tape, but the tape had peeled and the piece of bag had fallen, exposing a hole covered with a plush, dark green mold that spread a bit onto the pink tile around the hole. I took a bath and leaned away from the hole.

On Sunday morning, I left early. I didn't like the house. I didn't like being in it. I wanted to get home and take a shower. I wanted to ask Elaine, "What kind of man lives in a house like that?"

November 2003

By this time, I had told Elaine everything I knew about Trent—about the kicking at night and how his father had beaten him and how he held me so gently.

Sometimes Elaine pauses a bit before she answers a question. She may be waiting for me to settle down so that I can listen to what she has to say.

"People replicate how they feel about themselves in their surroundings."

I looked at her blankly.

"We already know he doesn't feel good about himself by the letter he wrote you. The house is his way of showing his internal misery."

"But he can fix anything. Why doesn't he fix the mold in the bathroom?"

"Because he doesn't think he deserves better."

I don't remember how the conversation went from there. I do remember wondering whether I was up for this, for being with a man whose insides must be moldy if that was what he was expressing in his outsides.

I decided to stay until I decided to leave.

The house at Mud Lake and Trent's father both made me feel the same way. They gave me the creeps. Something about them under the surface, something to fear or something that was feared. A violence was there, waiting to spring or already sprung.

I'm not weak. I'm not squeamish. I used to be the hospital dental hygienist at Hennepin County Medical Center, which is the county hospital in Minneapolis. One-third of my patients were Vietnamese and Cambodian refugees, one-third were people too ill or too contagious to be treated in a typical dental office, and one-third were inmates at the Hennepin County Jail.

Most of those prisoners were just like any patient in a typical dental office, but with a few of them I was wary, on guard, always keeping in mind a way out, an escape plan. I have been up close with violent men who were not subdued by the chains around their wrists and feet. I have cleaned their teeth. I was on guard with them and with Trent's father. I was the same way with Trent's house.

It shouldn't have been that frightening. It was nothing more than a dated ranch, worn with time, losing its fight against the Mud Lake mud, mud with particles so fine they permanently stain everything they touch. I confessed this to Trent—that his house (not his barn, never his barn) made me feel uneasy. He blew me off. I thought he was dismissing me, but I think he was waiting to be sure I was ready to hear the story.

It was months before he let me go down into the basement and then only because he needed help. The basement had flooded again. I noticed the mold growing up the 2×4s and the rusted high-water marks on the washing machine and dryer—indications of previous battles lost.

Trent worked the wet-vac and I the squeegee, working the rubber blade at the end of the long wooden handle to send water Trent's way. When we came back upstairs, wet and exhausted and disheartened, I told Trent again that being in the basement bothered me and that it had little to do with the water. He got a beer, poured me a glass of wine, and settled back in one of the captain's chairs to tell the story. Even if a story was unpleasant, Trent enjoyed the telling.

In the 1960s and 1970s, the people who owned the house boarded wounded Vietnam veterans in the basement—four of them. The owners got money from the government for housing the veterans. They also ran a pig farm and that's what Trent figured the vets ate—a lot of pork.

I imagined it and pictured wounded vets in the basement in wheelchairs. I hadn't seen any evidence of a wheelchair-accessible exit.

"How did they get outside?"

He took a pull on his beer before he answered.

"I don't think they did."

I learned this in 2005. In 2006, to sell the house, Trent stripped the basement bare, pulling out every piece of moldy wallboard and every 2×4. He tore an old poster off the wall—a poster that had always looked out of place to me. When it was gone, I realized it was there not because of what it showed but because of what it hid. Behind it was an elaborate portrait of a man drawn in blue ball-point pen. The man had muscled and tattooed arms crossed against his chest, long hair that rested on his shoulders, a firmly set mouth, and eyes that looked like they were screaming.

When Trent painted the basement, he painted over the portrait but it kept leaching through the paint. Trent said he had put four or five coats over it but it still kept bleeding through. He asked me if I knew anything that would work, and I told him that on a very small line of ink I had used clear fingernail polish and it did work. Trent wasn't about to fingernail-polish over the portrait. He finally got it covered up, after, as Trent said, "enough paint to suffocate the motherfucker."

I'm willing to bet that anyone going into the basement of the house at Mud Lake will see a faint blue ink haze seeping through the paint and will feel like the ink is screaming.

December 5, 2003

I was going back to Trent's for the weekend but was smarter this time. I brought bottled water because the water at Mud Lake smelled rotten. I brought shoes that I wouldn't mind wrecking in the mud that surrounded the house. I brought rags to wipe Charlie's paws. I brought a corkscrew.

Sitting on the toilet, I looked around the room. Horrible pink tile everywhere. Window to my left with dead flies in the screen. Clean mirror. Tube of toothpaste on the counter. One adult and one child-sized toothbrush nearby. Wastepaper basket by my feet. I looked at the rounded white balls in the wastepaper basket.

I joined Trent in his bed wondering how to phrase my question. I decided to leap in.

"When did Jenna get her period?"

"She doesn't have her period. She's only ten years old."

"So what woman was here?"

Trent paused before he answered.

"Jane."

With a hole in my stomach, I realized that the odd smell I had been smelling, at first in the background but now in the foreground, was Jane's perfume on the pillow. I went weak inside.

"When?"

"Thanksgiving."

"When did she leave?"

"Yesterday."

"Did she sleep here?"

"Yes."

"On this bed?"

"Yes."

"On these sheets?"

Before he could finish his "Yes," I was out of the bed, wearing my T-shirt and nothing else. Trent tried to reassure me.

"She slept on the sheets but I slept on top."

"I don't care! I won't sleep on these sheets. I won't—"

By this time, I was crunching against the far wall, pulling down the bottom of my T-shirt, trying to un-naked myself. I was crying.

I stayed there as Trent changed the sheets. I didn't help him, didn't move until he had put back the green wool blanket. He asked me to lie down next to him and I did, only because it was late and I wasn't sure I could get myself home safely and I didn't know where else to go. I lay down stiffly, and for the first time didn't want to be next to him. I left early the next morning.

9. Notes

November–December 2003

There must have been some apology. I do remember that we slipped into a routine. On alternating weekends, Trent and I were in Michigan. On weekdays, we were in Chicago, Trent maintaining or fixing something overlooked by previous owners because it hadn't been urgent.

When I left for work, I frequently left Trent a note. When I came home, he had frequently left one for me. Usually they were light-hearted, but not always. Trent took one note I had written him, turned it over, and wrote on the back.

Things I appreciate about Jule:

1) She is honest with me.

2) She doesn't question me about the way I do things but gives me support.

3) She keeps herself clean, neat and always beautiful.

4) She is a good cook!

5) She is strong enough to hang with me on the creek.

6) The love I feel every time she touches me.

7) She has given me a chance to be part of her life.

I brought up number five to Trent many months later.

"You were testing me! When you took me canoeing in the snow and the ice-cold water—that was a test!"

"You gotta be strong if you want to hang with Trent Price."

Somewhere during this time Persephone asked me how it was going with Trent. I said that I liked him a lot but . . . I hesitated. "His grammar isn't very good."

Persephone was aghast, "Are you serious? You have doubts about a relationship because of grammar?"

December 13, 2003

It was a Saturday morning and we were at Mud Lake. Trent was making pancakes as I sat and watched. I had never really paid much attention to men's behinds before—I had tended to notice shoulders and backs. Trent's was particularly eye-catching, though: strong legs rising up to rounded and firm buttocks thinly covered in white briefs.

I thought back to the night before.

As I watched him tend to the pancakes, I decided that it would be fun to return the favor. Getting a pillow from the living room, I dropped it at his feet. He said nothing for a while, but then, suddenly, "Watch the pancakes."

With that he fell to the floor.

"What's wrong?"

"Nothing. I got dizzy. I'll be all right."

"No, I don't think this is normal. We should go to a doctor."

"No."

Trent won that time. I won the next. Being dizzy wasn't normal, I told him. Most people don't have headaches every day. He explained that he'd had them as long as he could remember. His first memory was when he was three years old. He had taken a belt and cinched it around his head to try to make the pain go away. His parents had taken him to a doctor but nobody could figure out what was wrong or how to fix it.

I dragged him out to Naperville. Because his blood pressure was 150/94, the doctor prescribed anti-hypertensives. He also did a brain scan to try to find an anatomical reason for the headaches, but the scan didn't give any clues. Trent was good about taking the medication and his face no longer looked pinkish all the time. But he still had headaches almost every day.

December 19, 2003

When I got home from work on Friday night, the man standing in the kitchen looked like Trent but not exactly. He was redder, his arms made wild gestures when he talked, and he moved clumsily. He leaned against the counter so that the counter could hold him up.

I accessed my mental breathalyzer—the one I depended on for safety growing up. Was Dad drunk on beer, or martinis, or—the worst—Jack Daniel's? What was Trent drunk on? Beer, yes. But more—something that made him angry, reactive, like a cornered wild dog. I decided that whatever it was, it was the Jack Daniel's equivalent and I needed to be careful. I wouldn't get any closer than his arm length plus six inches. I wasn't afraid he would hit me. I was afraid he would fall on me. I started with a softly spoken question.

"What's wrong?"

"Nothing."

"You're acting different. You don't seem like you."

"This is me. This is all me."

"You seem really drunk."

"I'm not drunk."

"Really? You expect me to believe that? You can hardly stand up."

"I'm fine."

"Well, whatever version of fine this is, I don't like it."

"Fine by me."

"Whatever."

I'm not sure where the conversation would have gone from there. It went nowhere because Trent fell down. I didn't see it happen because I had turned to walk away. When I heard the sound, I turned back to him.

He was slumped against the cabinets. He was crying.

"I don't want to go."

"Go where?"

"To Jane's. I don't want to."

"So don't. Stay here. Don't go."

"I can't. I have to go."

"What do you mean 'have to'? You don't have to go anywhere."

"She's expecting me."

"So what? Don't go. Break up with her."

"I can't."

"Can't or won't?"

"I can't."

"You're a grown man. Don't tell me you can't."

"I can't."

I started to get up to walk away when he said, "I can't because of Jenna."

That brought me back.

"What do you mean—you can't because of Jenna?"

"Jane is taking Jenna and me to New York for New Year's and if I break up with her she won't take us. I can't do that to Jenna. She wants to go so bad."

I slumped beside him, both of us needing the cabinets to stay upright. I held him. We sat there. Trent called Jane and told her he was too drunk to drive. When the floor and the cabinets got too uncomfortable, I made him stand up and walked him to bed.

The next morning, when Trent got up and left to go to Jane's, I pretended to be asleep. After he was gone, I saw the note he left on the counter. He wrote it on the back of a Jewel-Osco receipt for 750 ml of holiday eggnog and a thirty-pack of Icehouse.

> What do you do when you're in love? Hold them touch them, let them know how you feel. Be with them. Don't overdo it. If they love you too you will know. If you have one love in your life you are the luckiest fucker that ever lived.

December 2003

Before Trent left to go to New York, I gave him a coin to keep in his pocket. It was the Sacagawea one-dollar golden coin. It could stay in his pocket, I told him, and he could reach in and feel it to remind himself that he was making the trip for Jenna. Just like Sacagawea was taking care of her baby, he was taking care of Jenna.

They left on December 30. On that day, from Kalamazoo, Trent put a birthday card in the mail for me. It arrived on my birthday, January 3, when Trent and Jane and Jenna were in

New York. That it was a Mickey Mouse card made me smile but I cried anyway.

January 2004

I didn't talk to Trent when he was in New York. It was as if he disappeared into one black hole and I disappeared into another. They flew back on January 8.

When he came in through the back door, we just looked at each other. I don't know what I looked like. He looked a way I'd never seen him look before. It was as if someone had turned his volume down from eleven to almost zero. He didn't grab a beer from the fridge. I couldn't read him.

"How did it go?"

"I didn't have sex with her."

I didn't know what else to say or ask. I felt as if any potential step would touch a landmine so I said nothing.

"She grabbed me when I was taking a shower. I didn't do anything and she said, 'What's wrong with you? What the fuck is wrong with you?'"

I had expected Trent to break up with Jane after New York, but he didn't. I thought about telling him that I couldn't take it anymore and telling him that he had to choose, but I didn't.

One of the rules I made for myself when I first learned about Jane was that I wouldn't force him to choose. I was the late entrant into the triangle. I was the one who knew what I was getting into. I was the one who would wait. There would be a rainbow at the end of the ledge. But there wasn't. There was just more ledge.

10. Crowded

January 2004

Because of the nightmares and the kicking and the headaches and waking up every morning wanting to kill himself, I had tried to get Trent to see Elaine. I was looking for something or someone that could make him feel better. He had refused.

One day, though, as I was walking out the door for my appointment, I joked that he was welcome to come with me if he wanted. He said he would. We sat stiffly on the couch opposite Elaine. He was stiff because he was wary. I was stiff because I wanted the session to go well.

Trent said almost nothing, so Elaine turned her attention to me.

When we left, I asked him what he thought. "She's all over it," was all he said. I had never heard him say that before so I wasn't entirely sure what he meant. I thought it was a positive reaction, but maybe not. Now I know that it was his highest form of praise.

Just before my next appointment, Trent said he would like to come along. My heart lifted. *He wants help! He wants to not want to kill himself!* Sitting on the small loveseat in Elaine's tiny waiting room, our feet nearly touching the table with the tea and coffee against the opposite wall, Trent surprised me again by asking if he could go in first and speak with Elaine alone. I was elated.

After a long time, Elaine opened the door and beckoned me in. I expected to once again sit on the couch next to Trent, but he stood up and left the room. Elaine closed the door behind him before she and I both sat down. She spoke first.

"Trent has something he wants you to know and he doesn't feel comfortable telling you himself."

I wondered—would this be about the headaches? Or about wanting to kill himself? I waited for Elaine to continue.

"There is something Trent would like you not to do anymore."

What? This was going to be about me? My stomach tightened as I prepared for difficult news.

"There are times, after you and Trent make love, that you make reference to your former husband. Trent would like you not to do that anymore."

"But I didn't . . . it was just that Trent made me feel so different, so good . . . I was only—"

I wanted to crawl into the couch, disappear into the gap between the seat back and the cushions. I had never been embarrassed in front of Elaine before, but I was now. Despite my protests, I had gotten her point and I wanted her to stop. She didn't stop; she made sure I understood what I had been doing and she cut me off to continue her lesson.

"A couple's bedroom should be a special place, a private place, just for the two of them. Whenever you talk about another person, whoever that person is, you bring that person into your bedroom with you. Do you really want to bring your ex-husband into the bed with you and Trent?"

"No."

"You'll want to think about this, not just regarding your ex-husband, but anyone. If a couple isn't careful, their bed can become very crowded."

Trent and I said nothing to each other as we left the building. When we got out to the parking lot, I thanked him for letting me know and I said I was sorry. He didn't say anything but he reached over and squeezed my hand.

11. Girlfriend

Early February 2004

Trent told me that he would like me to meet Jenna and wanted to introduce me to her as his girlfriend. He said that I was the only woman he had ever introduced to Jenna as his girlfriend.

"What about Jane?"

"Nope."

"So what does Jenna think Jane is?"

"A friend."

I was dubious. Kids know what's going on. They always do. They are students of the people they depend on to stay alive. But I let it go.

We were going to meet in two Saturdays, on February 14. Trent had Jenna for Valentine's Day that year. Although I wasn't looking forward to spending Valentine's in a house with a moldy bathtub, I was looking forward to meeting Jenna.

I thought about the worn picture on Trent's keychain. Then I remembered that the photo was five years old. What would she be like—more like Trent or more like her mother? Would she like me? Would I like her? What do you do with a ten-year-old?

I had no frame of reference because I didn't have children and had never babysat anyone that age, just infants to about six or seven. After that, I don't know about them. I would just have to figure it out. And I wondered if Jenna was wondering similar things about me.

February 14, 2004

Charlie and I stayed at Mud Lake while Trent left to get Jenna. I sat in the living room on the green couch and looked out the big window and waited.

Trent drove ol' Betsy—his big faded-blue 1980s Chevy Silverado. Ol' Betsy had done the honor of hauling the float that held Jenna's Girl Scout troop in a Battle Creek parade. Jenna and Trent both loved ol' Betsy. So did I.

Ol' Betsy was the hardworking truck that had pulled down the fence, weakened the telephone pole, and hauled the dirt out of my backyard to make the drainage right. She hauled the old wood fence to the dump. She hauled the lumber to build the new fence. She hauled the bags of concrete. She was a tough truck, didn't complain, and wasn't ashamed about her looks. Trent had replaced her engine with something newer and more powerful. Ol' Betsy and Trent both knew what she could do.

The truck pulled into the driveway and Trent and Jenna got out, moving quickly against the cold. They came right in the front door (why the front door rather than the garage door that we typically used?) and Trent introduced us. He looked happy when he said the word "girlfriend" but mostly he looked happy just to be with Jenna.

I did what I always do when I meet kids—I bent down so we could be eye to eye and said hello. I think I reached out my hand and we shook hands. She had straight brown hair parted in the middle, Trent's broad forehead, wide-set brown eyes ringed with thick lashes, and a sprinkling of freckles across her nose. I had expected her to be tall but she wasn't.

Molly was there, too. Molly was Jenna's border collie and she was getting to know Charlie. Molly was smaller than Charlie by about half, but she had already established her dominance. She was bred to herd sheep, and it looked as if she was looking forward to herding Charlie. Charlie was simply happy to have a friend.

Jenna suggested we go outside and play in the snow. We pulled on our jackets, mittens, and hats. My hat was a fleece windblocker that came to a point at the top. Jenna's was a black knit hat with cat's ears at the top.

It was really cold that day. It had been warmer the day before, which had softened the snow, which now had a thick, hard crust. Jenna and I used our mittened fingers to cut shapes out of the crust. Sometimes our mittens would mash the shapes, so we fine-tuned the process by getting two large bolts from the barn to use as our cutting tools, sawing as if we were cutting a fishing hole through ice. I cut circles. Jenna cut squares but wasn't happy that the corners kept breaking off.

"You do it better than I do."

"What?"

"Yours don't break like mine."

"That's because I'm doing circles. No corners to break. Circles are a lot easier."

Jenna then did a circle and held it up for me to see. It didn't break. Then I did a heart and held it up for her to see. It didn't break, either.

Trent let us play together in the snow for a while and then came outside and joined us. Charlie spun from one of us to the other while Molly circled her flock. The humans, with encouragement from two wagging tails, decided to build a snow fort.

Jenna and I had started and were using our hands to pack the snow and build the walls. After a look at our meager progress, Trent left and came back with a big shovel. He shoveled snow to us and we packed it down to build up the walls. We got them pretty tall, almost as tall as Jenna. It was a good fort and had two round openings for entrance and exit. Jenna and the dogs had a blast going in one opening and out the other.

We went inside the house to get warm. Jenna made a cootie catcher and she and I played with it. Trent said we were having chicken, green beans, and mashed potatoes for dinner. "My favorite!" Jenna cried.

The next morning, Trent made his dippin' eggs, bacon, and toast. I watched him cook for us and thought that I had never seen him happier. I liked Jenna and I liked watching Trent with her. You could tell they had spent a lot of time together. Sometime that weekend, we watched *The Blair Witch Project*—not the real movie but a reenactment, starring Jenna and one of her friends, with Trent as the bad guy.

Trent had chased the girls around the tree out front and the girls screamed. They shot the video after sunset so it was dark and grainy and might even have been scary except that after every scream, the girls laughed.

12. Disbelief

February 18, 2004

I got home from work and Trent was unsteady, leaning on the kitchen counter. I recognized it this time. I didn't like the look on his face and I was on guard. He was ready with his accusation.

"You're just going to go back to him."

"What?"

"Don't act like you don't know. You know what I'm talking about."

"No. I don't."

"You're just going to leave me and go back to your ex-husband."

I thought about how to answer that in the plainest way, to make my utter detestation of that idea completely clear to a drunk man.

"I'd rather be homeless than go back to him."

"Bullshit."

I was surprised that he didn't believe me. I didn't know what else to say. I do remember that somewhere in this conversation I sat down on the kitchen floor.

"I could have him killed," Trent said.

"What?"

"Your ex-husband. I could have him killed."

"Are you being serious?"

"Absolutely. I know people who could do it."

Trent knew all kinds of people and I decided that, yes, he probably did know people who could do it.

"No. Please don't do that."

"You don't want me to do it because you still love him."

"No, I don't. I just don't want you to go to jail."

"I wouldn't go to jail. I could have him killed and no one would know I was behind it."

"Please. Just forget about this."

"You want me to forget about it because you still love him."

"I do not. And I don't want you to go to jail."

"I told you. I wouldn't go to jail."

"I don't believe you."

"You don't believe me because you don't want him dead."

"Actually, I don't care one way or the other if he's dead or not."

"Really? You don't care if he's dead? You want me to have him killed?"

"No, I don't want you to have him killed. I want to stay with you and have everything be fine."

"If he's dead everything would be fine."

"This is hopeless."

"Tell me you want him killed or I'll know you still love him."

I weighed my options. I hoped these were the ravings of a drunk man and that this would all pass by morning, when the alcohol had worn off. I pictured myself on the witness stand saying, "But he was so drunk, I didn't think he really meant it." I decided to push.

"You're telling me no one could trace it to you?"

"No one."

"Then go ahead. Have him killed."

Trent gave me a long look. I hoped I had judged correctly.

The next night Trent brought it up again, but he wasn't as drunk this time. "You're just going to leave me and go back to him." I told him that this was his idea, not mine, that he was still thinking about my ex and I wasn't. I told him that I would bring him something tomorrow so he would have proof that I was never going to leave him and go back to the man in the purple suspenders.

The next day I went to work and it was the first thing I did. I wrote it quickly and stood by the printer as two copies printed out. I took them home and we each signed and dated both copies. It was a contract.

> I, Jule Kucera, being of sound mind and body, do hereby solemnly swear that I will not go back to the man with whom I was formerly involved.
>
> I will not go back because Trent Allen Price has shown me how it is supposed to be when a man loves a woman. He has shown me this by his integrity, his goodness, his kindness, his passion, and his tenderness, and by the way he holds me.

Trent never again brought up the subject. I don't know what happened to my copy, but I found Trent's in his top dresser drawer after he died. It had been folded to a size that would fit in a back jeans pocket. It looked like he had handled it more than once.

13. More Ledge

March 1, 2004

Trent had told me he needed to go to Jane's. I had forgotten that he was rehabbing her bathroom.

"Why don't you just break up with her?"

"I can't."

"Can't? Still can't?"

"Her birthday is coming. I won't do that to her."

"You weren't here for my birthday."

"I did that for Jenna and you know it."

The next morning, he came back from Jane's with a big smear of white first aid cream on his forehead. He had hit his head on the truck.

"Who put that there?"

"Jane."

I washed it off and put Neosporin on instead. I wasn't rough but I wasn't careful to be gentle.

March 2004

I was in the kitchen, washing my dinner dishes. Trent had said he would be back for dinner but hadn't shown up. He was at Jane's that day, working on her bathroom, either still working or . . . not. It was dark when he came up the back stairs, his steps heavy but quick. One glance at his face told me that he was angry. He said something negative about Jane.

"Sounds just like your mother," I blurted.

I turned quickly back to the soapy water. He didn't respond. Maybe he was considering the truth (or not) of what I had just said. Maybe he was looking for areas of similarity.

I don't know what he was thinking. I was thinking, If this is true, if there is some parallel between Jane and his mother, then breaking up with Jane isn't just about Jane, it's also about Jean. I decided that I might need to extend my time frame until the hoped-for-breakup to indefinite.

I do believe that first husbands and first wives and sometimes even the ones after that are people we select specifically and unconsciously because we are trying to work out some relationship issue with one of our parents. We are trying to make up for something that never was, win the love we never had, fix the thing that was broken, prove that we are good enough. But it is an old wound that the husband or wife or girlfriend or boyfriend cannot heal because it is too old and too deep. It can only be healed, or at least treated, from the inside.

I don't remember anything else about that night. I don't remember whether Trent got a beer out of the fridge (probably) or ate dinner (probably not), whether we talked (probably) or had sex (probably not). All I remember is keeping my head down and washing the dishes.

During this time of the triangle, I think it was the notes that Trent left that kept me staying. He started it, writing that first note after our first night, on the inside of the Schlage box that held the lock he was to install in the new fence. I wrote him notes, too, but mine were more restrained. So I waited.

April 2004

It was late and felt like the rerun of a show that I hadn't particularly enjoyed the first time. I was at the kitchen sink, washing dishes before going to bed. I like to do dishes—it relaxes me, especially when I am fretting about something. Trent was at Jane's. Once again I heard Trent's boots come up the back steps, heavy. I called a "Hello" when he came through the door but turned back to the dishes when I saw his face. He was angry again.

I know how to live like this—reading moods and deciding what action to take. I learned this growing up, on those nights when my father came home. I had lived like this again with the man in the purple suspenders.

It was like a card game with more than quarters at stake. The other person played a card and then, based on their card, I decided what card I would play. In this case I chose the "I'm not speaking until spoken to" card. Instead of speaking, I was thinking. I didn't like this role, this careful orbit around someone else. I didn't like how easily I slipped back into this role and how frequently I was playing it with Trent. I started to wonder whether it might be time to end the triangle, time for me to walk away.

Trent spoke, "I broke up with Jane."

I turned from the dishes. "How did it go?"

"Not good."

He looked more than angry. He also looked sad. I didn't know what to say so I just waited. After a few minutes and a little beer, he spoke again.

"She said mean things."

"Do you want to talk about it?"

"No. She made me promise I wouldn't tell you what she said."

I thought back to a conversation I had had with Elaine related to this. We talked about the wedge driven between a couple when someone else asks one of the two not to tell something to the other. It is a request that builds a wall.

Elaine and I had been talking about Jenna because Jenna wanted to share some secrets with me that she didn't want her father to know. I told Jenna, "If there's anything you don't want your father to know, then don't tell me, because your dad and I have an agreement to always tell each other the truth." Jenna wasn't happy with my answer, but it felt right to me.

I offered Trent the only solution I could think of. "Would you like to talk with Elaine about it?"

He thought about it and his answer may have surprised both of us.

"Yeah."

April 2004

The immediate result of Trent's breaking up with Jane was that the muscle spasm in his back went away. I took that as good news and as an indicator that other areas of difficulty in Trent's life would ease as well. I was wrong. The night kicking got even worse.

At Elaine's, we repeated the process we had used the first time, when Trent went in first and alone. When only ten minutes were left, I decided that this was going to be a solo session. But then the door opened, Trent came out, and I went in.

Elaine said that if I ever had any moments of doubt, if I ever wondered if Trent should have stayed with Jane and broken up with me, I could banish those doubts.

"I can tell you without question that Trent is better off with you."

"He is?"

"Yes."

"He said that Jane said mean things."

"She did."

And that was as much as either Elaine or Trent told me about the breakup.

When I had anticipated the end of the triangle, I had expected that there would be some drama that involved me. But all that remained was a faint mist, a chill on flesh, and the wobbliness of one leg of a stool suddenly gone. As pervasive as Jane had been, she was now, and would remain, completely absent.

Summer 2004

Sometime during that spring or summer, we acquired a turtle. His name was Ernest, Ernest T. Shackleton, named for Trent's favorite adventurer, but with Turtle as a middle name to distinguish him from Ernest Henry Shackleton, the polar explorer.

Trent found Ernest on the day he hatched at Mud Lake, when Ernest's drive for water mistakenly took him into the garage rather than the swamp behind the house. Ernest was so new he was rubbery. He was so small you could put him on a quarter with room to spare. Trent said he was a painted turtle, and that he would have bright-orange stripes along his head and neck when he was older.

Trent took a big white roasting pan and put some water in it. He set the pan on the dining room table and slid some papers under one end to create a baby-turtle-sized swimming pool, with a deep end at one end of the roaster and a white enamel beach at the other.

When Trent drove to Chicago to visit me, he would bring Ernest with him. Ernest rode shotgun in his white enamel car seat. He was a good traveler, Trent said, which was only to be expected since he was named after an explorer.

After Ernest got a little bigger, Trent got him an aquarium and set it up in the living room in Chicago. One day I thought it would be nice if Ernest had a little freedom, so I let him crawl around on the floor. After a few minutes, though, he started crawling oddly and I picked him back up and let him lie in my palm.

Something on the floor had poisoned Ernest. He was lying in my hand, not trying to crawl off as he normally would, staying in the center on my palm but twitching, all of his legs and his tail. I held him for a very long time and whispered over and over, "Please Ernest, don't die." He didn't, but as he grew his tail marked his age at the trauma with a sharp bend to the left.

Trent and I settled into a routine where we were in Chicago during the week and then in Michigan on the weekends. Every other weekend he had Jenna, and when he did, it would be the three of us.

With the exception of Saturday mornings, when Jenna did not like to get out of bed, the visits went smoothly. Trent got tickets to an overnight event at the Field Museum of Natural History. The sun was shining as we walked to The "L" with our arms full of sleeping bags and pillows. I felt light, and suddenly exclaimed, "We're having a family outing!" But then, because none of us had ever before used the word *family* when talking about us, I added, "Well, not a real family. But we're having an outing!" At that, Trent and Jenna simultaneously and emphatically said, "We *are* a real family."

I took those words, grabbed them from the air like falling leaves, and hugged them into my pillow and my sleeping bag all the way to the museum, all the way to the cold, hard marble floor where we laid out our sleeping bags in the spot that Jenna and Trent picked—in front of the tigers—all the way to lying down with Trent in the middle and Jenna and me on either side, all the way to the lights going out and listening to the breathing of my new real family.

14. Family Photo

July 2004

Not too long after the Field Museum excursion, my father and his girlfriend, Kaye, came to Chicago to visit on a weekend when Jenna was there. I like Kaye, now. I hadn't when they first started dating, when my father was sixty, I was thirty, and Kaye was twenty-eight. But they had been together almost twenty years and I was eventually able to see that my father had a much healthier relationship with Kaye than he did with my mother.

Jenna made little place cards for the table to indicate where we should sit and what we were going to eat. After dinner, at Kaye's suggestion, Trent, Jenna, and I banded together on one side of the table and my father took our picture. Kaye then took the camera and inspected the result. Declaring, "It's not very good," she then took several more.

About a week after my father and Kaye left, an envelope arrived with three color copies and three black-and-white copies of the best photos—a set for each of us. I appreciated that Kaye had thought to send the photos in triplicate. She understood the difficult practicalities of families who don't live together.

That photograph is the only picture ever taken of the three of us.

It's a nice one. Trent and I are sitting at the dinner table and Jenna is standing behind us, her head rising between ours, wearing the sweatshirt of a band that she loved then but can't stand now. Our faces are close together and we are all smiling broadly.

15. Bad Baby & the Prince

Summer 2004

Trent's night kicking was bad again. The stories of the nightmares varied but they were all the same at the core. Trent would tell me about the nightmare and when I said it seemed related to how helpless he felt as a child, he would tell me that he was to blame for how his parents treated him. I couldn't talk him out of this belief, even when I used Jenna as evidence.

"Is Jenna responsible for how you treat her?"

"Course not."

"If she was really bad, really really bad, would she deserve to be beaten?"

"No! I would never hit her."

"So why is it different with you? Why are you to blame for your father hitting you?"

"I was a bad baby. I had headaches and I cried all the time."

There was no reasoning with Trent on this, so I decided to write a story for him. It would be a story that made it clear that it wasn't the baby's fault.

To write the story, I would gather up the few bits that he had told me and weave them together: the rocks in his parents' backyard, his father's hatred, the recent wound that left the faint T-shaped scar on his forehead, and the day he and his high school girlfriend, Connie Sue, ran to her parents' house. I would also weave in the things Trent loved: eagles and water and sunshine and love itself. The idea for the names would come from *Tatsinda,* my favorite story as a child, as would the happy ending. I don't remember writing it; it came out quickly. I then put it aside for the right moment.

It was the next story we read after *Endurance.* Trent listened very quietly. At the end he said, "That's a good story, Sweet Baby."

After we had read it a few more times, he asked, "Would it be okay to change something in the story?"

"What would you like to change?"

"Bulgar shouldn't use a gun."

"Sure, Sweet Baby, we can change that."

Trent then specified exactly where the wound should go and the word I should use to describe the hit. I went back and made the changes, then printed the story and reread it. Trent was right. It was better. It was also prophetic.

PRINCE TARKTEN

Once upon a time, there was a faraway land with many provinces. Every province was a realm, and every realm was ruled by a king and queen.

King Tandor and Queen Talara ruled the realm of Trillium, which was one of the finest realms in the land. It had hills and streams and woods and many animals, and in the valleys, many farms. King Tandor and Queen Talara's castle had been built partway up one of the highest hills, with woods at the back and wildflowers at the front that blew in the soft wind and ended in the valley, at the banks of the wide river that ran the length of Trillium.

The castle was the finest building in the realm. When the sun rose each morning, it would cause the spires to sparkle like diamonds and the walls like sapphires. The royal flag with the royal crest flew from each spire; it was blue and gold and held aloft by the gentle breezes. The castle had four gates, one to the north, one to the south, one to the east, and one to the west. A pair of royal guards in their royal uniforms stood tall and proud on either side of each gate.

On this day at this time, King Tandor and Queen Talara were playing with their son, Prince Tarkten. They had married ten summers earlier, and had waited eight summers for a child. So when the prince was born, the king, the queen, and all the kingdom rejoiced. And on some mornings, such as this one, the king and queen delayed their royal duties to play with their son, and the sound of their laughter rolled down the hill and spread into the valley and prompted the birds to sing.

Everyone who heard them laughing smiled, except for Salmar. The king would not recognize Salmar but she would recognize him, from the cold day five years back when he had ordered the death of her husband for beating his wife, as an example to all the husbands in the kingdom. And although Salmar had hated her husband, she also missed him, and on this day she hated the king for taking her husband from her.

Salmar stewed in her hatred, her thoughts twisting in her mind. She stewed and stewed until her soul grew small and cold and twisted her in circles. She twisted and twisted until she became a spinning wind, and she began to blow through the valley.

Salmar blew herself across the valley, and the birds took shelter deep in the trees and wrapped their talons tightly around the branches. She blew herself up the hill toward the castle. She blew herself up the castle walls. She blew herself through the open window of the prince's room.

There was no laughter as Prince Tarkten was lifted by the spinning wind and blown out the window, blown down the hill, and blown into the river. Queen Talara screamed, "My son!" and King Tandor called for the royal guards.

They set out immediately, the king and the head guards on horses that had been rushed from the royal stables, the rest on foot. They galloped and ran down the hill to the river.

But Salmar was still spinning her wind and she blew sand and dust into the eyes of the men and the horses. As they struggled to find their way, the swiftly moving river carried the prince farther from them.

As Salmar was spinning and spinning, she saw everything. She saw Prince Tarkten floating away and she saw the king trying to get to the river and she saw the queen crying. And then Salmar began to cry, because she knew what she had done. She felt so horrible that she changed from wind to water, and she became tears that fell into the river. So Prince Tarkten was carried away by the river and Salmar's tears.

The king and the guards searched the river desperately. They broke into three groups: one to search the north bank, one to search the south bank, and one to dredge the river. They walked for miles and miles. They walked through weeds taller than a man and bushes and brambles and thorns. Mud pulled at the boots on their feet; thorns cut their hands. They did not stop and they would not stop. Every man looked for the king's son as if he were searching for his own, for that was their level of devotion to their king and that was their love for their sons.

They would have searched until they fell from exhaustion, but the river stopped them. They heard it first—the sound of a rushing waterfall, falling farther than four times as high as the highest spire of the castle from the ground. They looked over the edge and saw it churning and foaming, and they knew that no man, let alone a small child, could have survived the fall. And when the king saw it he wept and rent his robes in mourning.

Now no child could have survived that fall, but this was no ordinary child. This was Prince Tarkten, and sometimes special things happen to princes. What happened to this prince was very special.

Just as Prince Tarkten was going over the edge of the waterfall, he was seen by an eagle. The eagle dove and then leveled himself, spread his wings, and caught the falling prince. But the prince was much heavier than the eagle. The eagle held on as long as he could, until he saw a soft spot of grass at the riverbank, and he gently dropped the prince onto the fluffy mound.

But the weight of the prince dislodged the grass mound, and he was once again floating down the river. He floated for three days, tended to by the eagle, who splashed river water on his face so he had something to drink, and dropped berries into his mouth so he had something to eat, and flew over him, to shield him from the sun.

Trillium was not at war, but it did have an army and one troop was performing field practice. After a hard morning made harder by Captain Bulgar, they were taking a break. Some men were in the river gathering water in canteens and cooking pots; some were downstream from them, washing off the dust of the field. Captain Bulgar had separated himself from the men and had gone up the riverbank, upstream. He was relieving himself in the river when he noticed something floating toward him. When the mound of grass got closer he played a game, and he hit the grass with his yellow water, and was surprised when the grass cried.

The river carried Prince Tarkten right to the edge of the riverbank where Captain Bulgar stood. He looked and contemplated the child. He considered pushing it back with the toe of his boot, but then he remembered his wife, Phillify. She had been bothering him for some time about wanting a baby. He knew that would not happen because he did not desire his wife. This child could solve that problem. So he reached down and grabbed Prince Tarkten from the grass. And for the second time, Prince Tarkten cried.

Now the eagle had been hovering overhead, but hearing the prince's cry, he rushed to his defense. The eagle slapped his wings at the captain's head and scratched his face with his talons. But the captain simply drew his sword and pierced the eagle's heart. And so it was that the captain walked away from the riverbank with a crying child in one hand and a dead eagle in the other.

When Captain Bulgar gave the child to his wife, Phillify took it and smiled, but she was not happy. Although this was a son, it was not her son. She did not love it and she never would. But she did take care of the child, not because she wanted to, but because of her fear of Bulgar.

So it was that Prince Tarkten came to live in a cold house with Phillify and Bulgar, and they named him Rud. And over time Rud grew, and he grew big and strong.

As Bulgar watched Rud grow, he hated him. He hated the way he laughed. He hated how easily he could do things and build things. He hated his intelligence. But he found him useful. He used Rud to feel better about himself.

There are many sad stories that could be told, but we will tell only the last one, for to hear more than one is too difficult to bear.

When Rud was almost thirteen, Bulgar decided he needed a bigger house, and since he had been stealing goods from the army and selling them, he could afford it. He decided to build a large room onto the house he had. Phillify asked for the room to be built on the south side of the house, where it would be sunny and warm, but Bulgar only laughed. Bulgar wanted the room on the north side, where it was more visible and would impress the people of the town. But there was one problem—there were three huge rocks on the north side.

So Bulgar hired a man to remove the rocks. The man hitched ten horses to the rocks. But the rocks did not move and the man failed.

So Bulgar hired a second man to remove the rocks. The second man used timbers and levers, but the rocks did not move and the second man failed.

So Bulgar hired a third man to remove the rocks. The third man used special explosive powder. A small piece smaller than a loaf of bread broke off one of the rocks, but the rocks did not move and the third man failed.

Rud had watched the first man and the second man and the third man. And Rud said to Bulgar, "I will remove those rocks for three gold coins, one for each rock." And Bulgar snickered and agreed because he knew Rud would not be able to remove the rocks and because Bulgar took pleasure from watching Rud fail.

Rud decided to do his work at night because he knew that if Bulgar saw him it would make him angry. So Rud got up in the middle of the night and began to dig. He dug a great hole next to the largest rock. When it was big enough, he rolled the rock into it and covered it with dirt and laid the grass back on top of it. And then he went to bed.

The next morning, Bulgar was standing at the kitchen window, eating a fried egg. He blinked. Two rocks. There were only two rocks. He stormed out of the house.

The next night, Rud dug another hole, and the next morning there was only one rock.

On the last night, when Rud rolled the last rock into the last hole, he sat on the spot and smiled. He had done it. He had removed the rocks after three men had failed. And a small piece of his heart hoped that Bulgar would be proud of him. And then he fell asleep on top of the grass on top of the dirt on top of the rocks.

But the next morning, Bulgar was not proud, he was angry, for he felt that Rud had made a fool of him. And as he looked out the window and saw Rud sleeping happily, he was angrier. So he walked outside and kicked Rud awake. Then he threw the three gold coins hard at his face.

Now, something happened when the coins hit the prince's face, and he told Bulgar not to do it. But Bulgar could not be stopped and he took his hand and hit the prince's face over and over and over. And then the prince hit him back.

Now perhaps if the prince were sixteen or seventeen, he would have won. But he was not even thirteen, and even though he was big and strong he wasn't big and strong enough.

The second to last thing Bulgar did was pick up the piece of rock smaller than a loaf of bread (for it had not been buried with the others), lift it up over Rud, and let it fall on his forehead. The last thing Bulgar did was laugh. He left the prince bleeding and bruised on top of the grass on top of the dirt on top of the rocks.

Phillify had seen all this from her bedroom window but she did not move to help Rud. She knew what a beating from Bulgar felt like and she didn't want one. She didn't want anything she had, she didn't want to be where she was, so she pretended she was somewhere else. She closed her eyes and disappeared into her own mind.

But someone else had been watching. Nesula lived with her parents across the way from Rud and Bulgar and Phillify. She had seen everything and she had seen it for a long time. She waited until Bulgar had walked away up over the hill and then she ran to Rud, for she loved him. And she did not know it, but Rud loved her.

She got him up and carried him to his house and laid him on his couch. She washed his wounds with cool water and put a soft feather pillow under his head. When she had done everything she could think of and she could think of nothing else, she lay down beside him and wrapped her arms around him. And as they slept they both had sweet dreams.

When Bulgar came home and found them sleeping together, his blood grew hot and his eyes grew angry. He grabbed Nesula and threw her off Rud. Her head hit the wall and she slid to the floor. Rud awoke to the feel of Bulgar's coarse hands around his neck. Bulgar was trying to choke him. Bulgar was trying to kill him.

Rud fought back but he wasn't big enough, he wasn't strong enough.

Nesula opened her eyes and saw what was happening. Bulgar, in his anger, never saw her. He never saw her pick up the heavy frying pan. When the frying pan hit the back of Bulgar's head it was his turn to slide to the floor.

Nesula and Rud ran. They ran out of Bulgar's house and they ran to Nesula's house for safety. Nesula's parents were at the door and they swept Nesula into their arms. But when they saw Rud covered with bruises and the blood flowing from his forehead, they forbade him to enter. So Rud did the only thing he could. He ran.

He ran through fields and woods and brambles and thorns and he ached and bled and cried and fell exhausted at the river.

And once again the birds tended to the prince. They splashed river water on him to cleanse his wounds, to cool his fever, and to drink. They gently placed berries in his bruised mouth for him to eat. And at night when the sun fell and the air cooled, they covered him with their wings.

During the time that the prince had been lost and believed dead, the king and queen never forgot him. The queen shed three tears for him every morning, and the king and queen together said a prayer for his soul every night.

On the third night that the prince was sleeping and healing by the river, the queen had a dream. She dreamed of a glorious blue river, the sound of which was like the sound of many violins. A great bird arose from the river and spoke to her. "Your son is not dead. He is sleeping. He is sleeping the sleep of one who does not know who he is. You will find him by the river, where the eagles fly." And in her dream the queen responded, "But how will I know him? It has been eleven years and he was very small. I can hardly remember him." And in her sleep, a tear left her eye and rolled down her cheek. And the great bird answered, "Only royalty is permitted a name that begins with a T. His name has been lost, he does not know it, but a T marks his forehead. Go to him."

The dream woke the queen and the queen woke the king and at first light the search party departed, headed for the river, lifting their eyes to look for eagles.

Seven eagles led them to Prince Tarkten. They found him facedown, and they all held their breath as they turned him over. A T marked his forehead. It was left by the piece of rock smaller than a loaf of bread.

King Tandor and Queen Talara wept when they saw their son. The royal doctor examined him and ordered attendants to dress his wounds with rosemary oil and lay him on a bed of lavender. The king and queen never left his side; they touched him and held him and stroked his hair.

When he was well enough, Prince Tarkten sat up. When the king and queen told him who he was, he did not believe them and he laughed. But over time, he came to believe, and over time, he answered their questions about what had happened to him.

When the king learned what Bulgar had done to the prince he was outraged, for the law of the kingdom declares that anyone who strikes royalty shall be put to death. But when the king demanded that Bulgar be found and be put to death, Prince Tarkten said only, "No. Cut off his right hand, for that is the hand with which he struck me. And cut off his right large toe, for if he tries to strike anyone with his left hand he will lose his balance and fall." So that is what they did. And Bulgar did try to strike someone with his left hand and he did fall, and those around him laughed.

One night after a tasty meal of pheasant and venison and fruits from the fields, Prince Tarkten was thinking about how much his life had changed, and wondering how good it could get, how wide he could open his arms to receive good things. It was then that Queen Talara asked, "Tarkten, is there anything else you desire, anything else that would make you happy?" And the prince smiled, his eyes crinkled, and he asked, "Do you think the royal guards could find Nesula?"

On the day that they were married, Prince Tarkten wore a robe of royal-blue velvet and a crown of gold with diamonds and sapphires. Princess Nesula's robe was the color of the sky at dawn, her crown was gold, and diamonds and sapphires were woven into her hair.

After they said their vows, they kissed, and the birds of Trillium sang their pleasure. Then two white doves flew into the gathering, carrying a gold ribbon. Prince Tarkten and Princess Nesula followed the ribbon through the valley, through the woods, and into a clearing. It led them to their new home, their nest that was built for them by all the birds of Trillium. It had woods at the back and wildflowers at the front and gentle breezes that carried the sounds of their joy. Prince Tarkten took Princess Nesula into his arms and carried her over the threshold. They held each other and loved each other and told each other the truth. And Prince Tarkten and Princess Nesula lived happily ever after.

The End.

16. Trouble with a Capital T

Thanksgiving 2004

Trent made me promise to behave myself at his parents' house. I don't like either of them. He knew that and asked me to be polite to them, the way he was polite to mine. He asked me not to say anything that would make them mad, not for his sake, but for Jenna's. Trent wanted Jenna to have a good relationship with her grandparents.

Trent's father is Herb, his mother is Jean, and Jean's twin sister is either Joan or Joanne, depending on who is saying it. Her son Steven calls her Joan. Trent called her Joanne. Jean and Joanne call each other by the same name, Louie. Trent and Steven refer to them as The Twins. Confusing, at the very least.

As part of the Thanksgiving visit, Jean and Joanne took Jenna and me over to Joanne's house; they wanted me to see it. There were lots of black-and-white pictures on the wall—of Joanne and her husband when they were a young couple, of Gary and Steven, their two boys, when they were babies and little boys. I looked closely at the boys, trying to see the man that Steven had become and trying to tell what Gary was like, because he had been Trent's best friend, and because he had died in his late twenties. Joanne pulled out some old photos of Trent when he was little and showed them to me.

Jean glanced at the photos and remarked, "Trent was a handful of a child. Always getting into trouble. Trouble with a capital T."

She smiled when she said it but her tone was unkind. Jean had been saying unflattering things about Trent throughout the visit, and she continued with an unflattering story. I waited until she was finished. I could stand it for Trent and I could stand it for myself but I could not stand it for Jenna. So I spoke.

"Jean, I'd like to hear a nice story about Trent."

"What?"

"All afternoon you've been telling us negative stories about Trent. I'd like to hear something positive."

Her jaw went down and I could see her mouth like an O that someone had colored in with a dull crayon.

Joanne helped her twin out. "He did get himself caught in a tree one time, when he was climbing it, and he hung upside down."

At the time I thought Jean didn't like Trent because he was a messy boy, always playing in the dirt, shirt coming untucked, pants knees stained with grass, as he investigated all the things he saw crawling or growing. Now I think that what she didn't like was that he was a boy.

It was in its way a festering wound and I was trying to explore it, trying to find the source of the infection so that it could be cured and Trent could feel better. I probed into Trent's parents' history to understand.

Herb was the youngest of six boys. Most of them were dead. One lived in Colorado. That was Joel, the one Trent wanted to talk to. Trent wanted to see whether Joel could explain why Herb was the way he was.

My theory is that Herb's father beat him, because beaters are typically beaten themselves. Separately, we have learned that the more male babies a woman has, the more likely each successive male is to be gay. I wonder whether Herb was gay and hated that about himself. This is all my conjecture, not Trent's.

As for Jean, Trent told me what he knew about The Twins. When Jean and Joanne were born, their mother died. In their father's eyes, the twins had killed their mother. Their father took their three older siblings and remarried. He left the twins behind with his parents.

When Jean and Joanne were growing up, if they wanted to see their father, their grandmother would take them to town. They would stand outside the town bar so the twins could look through the window and see him there, sitting at the bar. Their grandmother didn't take them often because she didn't think it was good for them.

All this, I believe, is why Trent's mother hates men, and why she married Trent's father, because he hates himself, and why, when they had a little boy, the father beat the little boy and the mother let him know that he was a handful, that he was trouble with a capital T, and whatever he tried to do or be would never be enough.

17. Moving Forward

February 2005

Trent and I had been talking about finding somewhere new to live together, since I couldn't stand Battle Creek and he liked the events Chicago hosted but not the city. We had gone out with an agent to look at land in southwest Michigan, a decent driving distance from Chicago. The expedition was miserable in every way. We decided to try again, this time on our own. We went to see property that bordered the Black River, most of it on a rise above the river, but part included the steep slope down.

Trent was stomping through the snow to get a sense of the land as I picked my way down the steep embankment. "Be careful," he hollered, as I held on to the thin trees to slow my descent.

I stood on the frozen bank, shoved my cold, unmittened hands into my coat pockets, and listened to the gentle rippling sounds of the river. A sudden loud crack told me I wasn't standing on the bank but on ice over the river. The ice broke off and I landed on a little ledge in water up to my ankles.

Just as I was breathing a sigh of relief, a louder crack and this time the ice went out from under me and I went down. I was now on my back, arms splayed on the ice, the bottom half of my body up to my waist in the ice-cold river. It was moving fast and pulling at me and I told myself to lie still or the ice under my back might break away. I knew that if I was pulled off the bank by the river and pulled under the ice I would probably die, from either cold or suffocation.

The odd part was that I knew that Trent would come get me. Either I cried out when I went down or he heard the crack of the ice. Just as my coat—it was wool—was getting heavy with water, I felt a pull from my shoulders and I was out of the river and in the snow. I thought my coat had pulled me out but it was Trent, grabbing me by the shoulders.

I remembered the temperature because we had commented on it earlier—18°F. Trent told me to run up the hill and I did and he ran behind me. He said if I didn't run my clothes would freeze and I would have trouble moving.

On the way up the hill he said, "When we get to the car, we have to get all your clothes off." The urgency in his voice had nothing to do with desire and everything to do with danger. Two very good things were working in my favor. First, he had left the car running and the heat on. Second, in the back seat was a basketful of clean laundry.

My clothes were already stiffening as we pulled them off. I put on Trent's briefs, a T-shirt, his jeans (which left my ankles exposed because though Trent was taller by far, I'm all legs), and his sweatshirt. I got in the car and pulled on his thick Redhead socks as Trent turned the heater to full blast.

We drove out from the property and found a road back into town. Just as we got there, though, the car lost its power steering and brakes. An auto repair shop was closing for the night, but Trent slipped the mechanic some cash to stay open and fix the car.

On the way back to Mud Lake, we talked about how lucky we were. Lucky that I hadn't slipped all the way into the river. Lucky that Trent had heard me fall. Lucky that the car had broken down in town and not in the woods. We had been lucky, but I was apprehensive about future property-hunting expeditions with him.

Spring 2005

Spring is the best and the worst season at Mud Lake. It is the best because the swamp comes to life. It is the worst because the ground thaws and the mud comes to life, too.

Houses on either side of the road to Trent's house varied considerably. Some were well-kept with mowed lawns; others had a slab of plywood nailed over the front door and a dirt circle where the dog forever chained to the tree had tramped the earth bare.

The house across the street was filled with lawn decor: cars in various states of repair or disrepair, garbage piled high by the end of the driveway because they rarely had money to have it hauled away, and a target deer that had been shot so many times the head had been blown off and the beige foam of the neck was exposed. I always wanted to cover that deer with a blanket.

Trent's house had trees and a mowed lawn but the front entrance looked off. It wasn't until you used it that you realized what was wrong—the steps had sunk so that it was a big step up from the top step to the inside of the house. Almost everyone used the garage entrance instead.

If you walked between the house and the barn in the spring, you would get taller as the mud adhered to the soles of your shoes in layers and your shoes became platforms. You would stop walking to find a rock or a stick to scrape the mud off your shoes so you wouldn't fall off them.

If you did fall, even if you fell in the grass, you would have a mud stain on your jeans that would never come out. You would remember to never again wear your good jeans to Mud Lake.

Trent kept two types of underwear: the good ones, which were white boxer briefs, and the bad ones, which were former white ones with mud stains. If you fell or sat and got Mud Lake mud on your jeans, it would seep through the cloth and stain your underwear. You could wash your underwear a hundred times with OxiClean or bleach and it wouldn't matter. Mud Lake mud is tenacious. It will never come out.

When I first started going to Mud Lake, I brought good clothes and bad clothes but over time I learned to bring only the bad ones. I followed Trent's lead and stopped packing a suitcase. I brought in my clothes clean in a laundry basket and took them out dirty the same way. At first it seemed strange to pack my worst clothes but I got used to it.

I liked only one place in the house at Mud Lake, the same place Trent did—sitting at the dining room table, looking out the big window that looked out over the swamp.

The property was what was called a typical eighty, specifically acres, 1,320 feet wide and 2,640 feet deep. The narrow edge was against the road and it stretched back into the swamp, past the creek that twisted through the property. You could see farther than the land Trent owned—you could see across 320 acres, about two miles.

If you were outside, the swamp would feel damp on your skin, even in August. It had its own smell that didn't change too much with the seasons; it just got a little less pungent over winter. It smelled of wet and decay and grass and smoke and scrambled eggs. It smelled like the moment between death and life.

In the fall, in the morning, when the cool air hit the warm earth, steam would rise and lie across the swamp in indolent layers that curled away if you walked through them. The swamp steam mingled with the smoke that came from the woodstove in Trent's barn, mixing and thickening until the logs burned down and the fire burned out. What remained was a stale, smoky smell that melded with hair the way Mud Lake mud melded with cloth.

Trent walked every part of the swamp that he could walk and canoed every part that he couldn't walk. Even though the swamp played tricks on him, opening up a hole that he fell into up to his chest, stopped only by leveling his shotgun to bridge the hole, sucking Gary's handgun from Trent's holster, the gun that Trent had been given after Gary's death and Trent not finding it even though he looked for days in every place he had been, Trent loved the swamp. When I asked Trent why he loved the swamp, he said, "It's where life begins!"

Trent applied for a home equity loan so that he could have cash to fix up the Mud Lake house so that he could sell it. I knew he was applying for a loan but, having once processed university student short-term loans, didn't expect him to be approved and therefore didn't worry about it.

We were at Mud Lake when he came inside, grinning. "Sweet Baby, I got a loan and I don't even have a job!"

My heart sank.

18. Encounter

Summer 2005

It was dusk. I was at Mud Lake and decided to take a walk outside. Trent loved the swamp. I didn't. However, one part of Trent's property was higher, safely elevated from the mud. This small rise grew big oaks and small dogwoods that bloomed in the spring. I liked walking there.

I left the house out the back door and headed down the slope toward the swamp and the woods. When I got to the edge where the trimmed lawn met the tall grass, the wind picked up. In seconds, it was blowing hard. I figured it was the Indian spirit that Trent believed—partly because of something his accountant, also a psychic, told him—was there to protect him, sending me a message, so I spoke to him.

"Is that you?"

I was hit with a fat gust of wind, the kind of wind that pulls a car door from your hand. I figured the Indian was answering my question and that he wasn't happy with me, because Trent and I had been talking about selling the house at Mud Lake and moving in together.

I stood and faced where I thought he was, and yelled back. "Go ahead and blow. I know you love him. I love him, too. And you can blow all you want but I am not going to stop. I love Trent Price and I am not going to stop."

At that, the wind stopped blowing, which made me afraid. I turned and went quickly back up the slope into the house.

I told Trent about what happened, or what I thought had happened. Trent didn't say anything so I wasn't sure what he thought. But there was more to tell, so I continued.

"Trent, the Indian wasn't alone."

"He wasn't?"

"No. I got the sense that he had an animal with him."

"What kind of animal?"

"Like a wolf, but not a wolf, because it was his animal, his partner. It was like a combination of a wolf and a dog."

Now Trent looked at me more closely. "How big was it?"

"Big. As big as the biggest dog I've ever seen. But it wasn't a dog. It was a wolf-dog."

"What color was it?"

"Dark. Not gray like a wolf but darker. Almost black but not shiny black. He was big and dark."

"What was the animal doing?"

"Nothing. He was just standing by the Indian. By his right side."

Trent then told me that the description I had just given matched Otis, Trent's dog who was half-Akita, half-German shepherd, who would sometimes stand with his front paws on Trent's shoulders, his head above Trent's. Otis was buried behind the barn.

Otis

"Tell me about Otis."

"What's to tell?"

"Well, if that's Otis hanging out in your backyard, I think I should know something about him."

Trent's face looked dark and I couldn't read it—was he angry? Was he sad? I waited but Trent said nothing so I figured I would start at the beginning.

"How did you get Otis?"

"At a fair. Not a fair with rides. An exotic animal fair. Snakes and lizards and other unusual animals."

"And that's where Otis was?"

"Yeah."

"Was he a puppy?"

"Not a little puppy but young, still small."

"What made you decide to get him?"

"I could tell he would be a good dog, good out here."

Trent didn't say more so I found another question. "How did you pick Otis for his name?"

Trent smiled briefly at the memory. "I was at work, taking the elevator up, and I looked down and it said, 'Otis.' Seemed like a good name."

That was all Trent offered so I decided to go right to the ending. I asked it as gently as I could, "How did he die?"

Something changed . . . the pressure of Trent's fingers on his Icehouse can increased or the flesh around his eyes tightened. Something told me this was going to be a hard story.

"Otis was a big dog. He used to hang out at the end of the driveway and stand with his paws on the fence. Standing like that he was a head taller than me. An asshole neighbor decided he was going to play tough with Otis, and Otis bit him."

Trent took a pull on his beer. "In Michigan, a dog is allowed one bite. If the dog bites a person a second time, the dog has to be killed."

Trent paused and I waited, a long time, while Trent opened the door to the story and prepared himself to go inside.

"We were having a party for Danielle [Jenna's half-sister] with some of her little friends. They were playing with dolls and stuff. Otis was chained up out back so he would be away from them. I told them, 'Stay away from the dog.' I was clear. 'Don't go near the dog.'"

His eyes moved back and I could tell he was seeing that day.

"It started snowing and I went out to the barn to get the woodstove going. One of those little girls looked out the window and saw Otis getting snowed on and she felt sorry for him. She walked down to Otis and she took her sweater off and put it over his shoulders. She didn't want it to come off so she tied the sleeves around his neck, and that's when he bit her. The police came and said Otis had to be put down. They didn't want to say it, either, but it's the law. Otis had to be put down."

Trent took a long pull on his beer. He was finished.

"Oh baby," I said, as I crawled into his lap and wrapped my arms around him. "I'm sorry," I said as I held him.

We stayed that way a long time. I was measuring, measuring just how many sad things one life can take, how much loss one heart can hold. In the balance of easy and difficult, love and hate, pain and pleasure, how long can a person stand on the side of difficult and hate and pain? I was measuring and I was trying to put some weight on the other side of the balance.

Framing O.T.

I asked Trent whether, for his birthday present, we could reframe the two photographs of O.T. that hung on the living room wall in the Mud Lake house. He liked the idea. O.T. had been Trent's great-uncle, Jean's uncle. As a child, Trent and his two cousins had stayed with O.T. every Sunday. For lunch, O.T. would make them a sandwich and, on the side, a round scoop of cottage cheese on a fluffy lettuce leaf with two cherries for eyes and part of a pineapple slice for a mouth. O.T. loved to hunt, but I think he was a hunter like Trent who didn't enjoy killing. O.T. did not wear camouflage when he hunted. Instead, he wore a red-and-black-plaid Woolrich hunting coat. I'd given Trent a coat like that for Christmas.

We went to my favorite framing store in Chicago and I showed Trent the display on the wall where the same picture had been framed ten ways, each frame changing the picture, either a little or a lot. We took our time walking along the two walls displaying frames—wood and metal, wide to narrow, dull to brightly colored. Our first decision was easy: wood, not metal. At a large table, an assistant carefully removed the photos of O.T. from their frames and their mats. She then pulled out several different frames so we could compare options. As she slipped each one over a corner of one of the photos of O.T. (the one with the shotgun), I could tell by Trent's expression that none of them looked right to him. Trent said he wanted to take another walk along the walls of frames. I followed.

"What about this one?"

It had a vine carved into it and was more delicate than what I thought Trent would pick. The narrower molding would require a narrower mat. The framed photos would be much smaller. We walked back over to the table. The assistant drew out a soft gray mat and placed it against the photo, then laid the vine frame next to it. Trent nodded, then turned to me for my opinion.

"It's perfect."

19. Sleepless

Late Summer 2005

I couldn't sleep.

We were at Mud Lake, the phone had rung the day before until Trent angrily unplugged it, and earlier in the week I had made Trent's most recent mortgage payment.

It was about six in the morning. I went to the dining room and found something to write on, one of Trent's many white legal tablets with the thick blue lines. Routing through the overstuffed pen cup, I finally found a functioning writing implement, a number 2 pencil with a hard eraser.

I drew a line down the middle of the page, planning to list monthly expenses on the left and income on the right. On the left side I first put mortgage payment, which used to be about $700 but with his home equity loan was now double that. Everything else I estimated: electricity, fuel oil, phone, gas, food, and child support. Then I tallied. I had a rough idea of what he was making from the work renovating an electrician's house and put that number on the right. I couldn't think of any other income. The number on the right wasn't large enough.

Trent found me staring at the numbers, and sat in the captain's chair beside me.

"What are you doing, Sweet Baby?"

"Figuring out why I couldn't sleep."

"Why couldn't you sleep?"

"Because of the numbers."

I showed Trent the paper. He corrected the amount for child support.

"And you don't even have beer on there."

"How much is that?"

"A thirty-pack is $12.99. So thirteen times ten or twelve."

I had no idea he drank that much. It seemed that we were accounting in several areas. I did the math and added $150 to the expenses and revised the total. The number on the right was now $700 too small.

"Trent, this is a hole."

"No shit."

"You were breaking even before the home equity loan but now . . . you can't cover this."

"Tell me something I don't know."

He stared at me and I stared back. He was trying to tell me something but he wasn't going to say it. I thought for a while and then it hit me.

"You knew you wouldn't be able to cover it."

He didn't say a word so I knew I was on track.

"Why would you take out a loan you knew you couldn't repay?"

He stared at me hard and I knew I'd have to figure this one out, too. Again, the answer came. This answer felt worse.

"You took out the loan because you didn't think you'd have to repay it."

Trent looked down. I was right. But still I was the only one talking.

"What were you going to do when they came to foreclose on the house?"

Trent lifted his head and his eyes met mine.

"Go down to the basement with two tanks of propane, take a seat by the fuel tank, and light a match."

He wasn't kidding.

Foreclosure

Most people who want advice regarding imminent foreclosure would probably see their accountant or lawyer. I saw Elaine. She and I talked about debt and the strain and the need for me not to sink my own boat while trying to get Trent to dry ground. I used Elaine as a checkpoint: was Trent, with these problems, worth it? Or was I once again sinking myself into not just a losing proposition, but a loss of myself?

I thought he was worth it and she agreed. As she pointed out, this time I was with a man who loved me, who would give up the world for me.

My plan was to sell the Mud Lake house quickly, have Trent move into the Chicago two-flat with me, live there for a couple of years and save money, then find a house in Michigan and move there.

When Trent and I saw Elaine together and Elaine asked Trent about living in Chicago, his whole body slumped. The way he spoke changed. The suffocation he felt when he was in the city was all over his face and his answer. I made an appointment to see Elaine by myself.

I was barely seated on her yellow leather couch when the words tumbled out of me.

"He can't do it. He can't live in the city."

"Anytime Trent is in a confined space he feels vulnerable. It brings back all those feelings from his childhood when he was in real, physical danger."

"My plan was for us to live here for two years, but that's not going to work. He won't make it."

Elaine said nothing and I just sat there. Then the realization hit me.

"I have to sell my house."

The Loan

Trent's plan had been to use the home equity loan to totally rehab the Mud Lake house, put it on the market, and get top dollar. When it became clear that the investment needed exceeded his available funds, he scaled back his renovation.

Trent went to the hardware store and came home with two new toilet seats and three new doorknobs. I thought the doorknobs and toilet seats were pointless, given the moldy fist-sized hole in the pink bathroom tile, the worn pine cabinets in the kitchen, and the plywood floor in the dining room, but I bit my tongue.

We decided that as soon as Trent had eradicated the mold from the bathroom and the basement, he would put the house on the market. Instead of coming to Chicago during the week, Trent stayed at Mud Lake and spent his days in the basement removing damp, moldy paneling, hauling it outside, and burning it. Then he scrubbed everything with bleach, several times.

When I visited over the weekend, the walls did look better after being scrubbed and painted, but a telltale line of rust on the washer and dryer at the high-water mark remained. I doubted a quick sale.

Trent worked with an agent and put the house on the market for less than he had planned but for more than I thought it was worth. The value was in the land, he said. I hoped he was right. I wasn't sure how many people wanted eighty acres when most of it was wet.

Trent came to Chicago. We went back one weekend and when we walked in through the front door, the back door was wide open. Trent angrily said something about fucking real estate agents and I walked across the dining room to shut the door. As I closed it, something seemed not right. I looked at the lock, opened the door, and then looked at the lock from the other side.

"You put the lock on backward."

"What?"

"The lock. The key side is on the inside, not the outside. It doesn't lock people out of the house, it locks people in the house out of the swamp."

Trent swore again and I almost cried. The lock was the physical equivalent of a Freudian slip. How would this man ever willingly leave this land?

A Ticket

Just after Trent finished clearing out and painting the basement, it rained hard and the sump pump failed. We got to the Mud Lake house late Friday night to find the basement flooded.

We spent most of the weekend in the basement, once again, Trent with the wet/dry Shop-Vac and me with the huge squeegee. I grew blisters on my hands and was glad to leave on Sunday. Trent stayed behind, in case it rained again. An open house was scheduled for Tuesday.

The agent was disappointed with the turnout. I can't remember whether only one or two people showed up or no one did. Word had already gotten out. The house or the land wasn't worth the drive to see it.

Later that week Trent called, sounding worse than he had after the open house.

"What's wrong?"

"Nothing."

"You don't sound like it."

"I got a fucking ticket."

"A ticket? For what?"

"'Illegal lane usage.' Fuck that. That's how you get your mail out in the country. You drive up to the box, no matter what side of the road it's on."

"You got a ticket for driving on the wrong side of the road to get your mail?"

"It's not the wrong side. It's how you do it in the country. It's how everybody does it. Fucking cop."

"'Illegal lane usage' doesn't sound that bad."

"Wouldn't have been if that's all it was."

"What else?"

"DUI."

It felt as if the hole we were trying to claw our way out of was getting bigger, that the basement and the swamp were filling with black muck and pulling us down, down so that trying to move our feet or arms made a sucking sound and after a while we'd have no fight left in us and the muck would cover us and we would disappear.

I was afraid Trent was taking me down with him.

20. Sad Eyes

Fall 2005

Over the summer, my dog Charlie, the elderly standard poodle, had started to fail. At first he merely stumbled going down stairs. The stumble, though, became a full-on slide down the steps as I pulled on the leash to keep him from crashing. When he ran full-bore into a closed door, I realized he was as good as blind. That was confirmed when we took walks and he would hit his head on things along the way.

His mind was next. I think he was flashing back to his early life in Texas, when he had been caged and starving. I would come home to see that he had eaten something, anything, all sorts of odd things, food and not food. I could never figure out what made him select a particular item. I assumed this happened during his "freak-out times," when his eyes went wide and he spun and ran and crashed into something and then attacked it.

I watched my next-door neighbor carry his aged golden retrievers up the two flights of stairs to his two-flat. I couldn't do that. Not a sixty-pound dog. I could manage to keep him from sliding down the stairs but I couldn't carry him back up. I thought about having Charlie put down. Trent and I had a long talk. All that matters is that Trent offered and I took him up on it. It was time.

We decided to do it at Mud Lake and bury him in the swamp. The plan was to dig the hole, put Charlie in it, shoot him, and then bury him. Trent paid the teenager across the street $20 to help dig the hole. It took a long time to dig the hole because it's hard to dig mud that clings to your shoes and your shovel. It was raining. I stayed in the house.

When Trent came in the house to get his gun, I offered to do it instead.

"He's my dog. I should do it."

"Have you ever taken a life?"

"No."

"You don't know what it's like. I'll do it."

I heard the shot. Then a second shot. That was all.

When Trent came in he went right to bed and I lay down beside him and held him. He was crying.

"He knew what I was going to do. I could see it in his eyes."

"I'm sorry."

"He just kept looking at me. His eyes were so sad."

I didn't say anything more. I just held Trent and felt guilty.

No Offers

People came to look at the house at Mud Lake but no one made an offer. Jenna said her classmates said it was because the price was too high.

Trent decided to sell his tractor. It was an antique and he was asking $5,000. He'd been offered $3,000. The stakes were high. The $5,000 would cover past due loan payments that would keep the house at Mud Lake out of foreclosure but the $3,000 wouldn't. Trent demanded $5,000 from the potential buyer and got it—the night before the day the house would have been turned over to the bank.

It was a tough time for Jenna. She wrote Trent a letter about how bad I was, making him sell his truck (which I did not do) and their home (which I was encouraging him to do). One night they screamed at each other for so long that I went outside to take a walk and came back in only because I got too cold. They were still yelling when I returned. I walked straight into the bedroom, closed the door, and pulled a pillow over my head.

It wasn't all hard. We still had banana pancake mornings and I still woke up to hear Trent tell me he loved me. Most of the time, though, it was hard. I stopped making mortgage payments for him. It was a question of which would come first—an offer or foreclosure. There were no more antique tractors to sell. Trent dropped the price.

The Piebald

Trent was in Michigan and I was in Chicago. When we spoke on the phone that night, Trent sounded especially happy. I asked him about it.

"Are you . . . happy?"

"Yeah."

"I'm glad. How come?"

"I danced with the piebald."

"You what?"

"The piebald. I danced with the piebald today."

The piebald was a deer Trent had been seeing at Mud Lake. I had never heard of a piebald deer until he explained. A piebald has white on its body as well as the tail. They can be all white or splotched with white. The white is caused by a recessive gene rather than parasites or disease. Generally piebalds have brown heads and white splotches on their body, but the one Trent had been seeing had a white head and shoulders and a brown body. Piebalds are rare and this coloration was rarer still.

The deer-hunting community has two schools of thought about piebalds. One believes they should be killed to preserve the genetic purity of brown deer. The other considers them special, but differs on how to treat that specialness.

Most think the specialness would make a great trophy hanging on the wall. The minority think the specialness should be protected. Trent was in the minority. More than that, Trent thought the piebald was a sacred being honoring his land by choosing to live there.

"How did you dance?"

"He was by the pine tree, the little one by the driveway. We just kind of looked at each other. Then I stepped toward him and he went around the tree. Then I turned around and he went the other way. It was like we were dancing together around the tree."

"Cool. Then what?"

"We stopped and looked at each other. Then he ran back into the brush toward the woods."

Thanksgiving

A few weeks before Thanksgiving, Trent told his mother that he and Jenna wouldn't be coming to her house for Thanksgiving dinner. He said he was forty-three years old and was going to have his own Thanksgiving in his own house. His parents were invited; he wouldn't be coming to their house.

Trent's mother told him he was being selfish. She said he was ruining the family tradition. She made her case and Trent held to his.

It was looking as if Thanksgiving was just going to be Trent, Jenna, and me, but the day before the holiday, Jean called and let him know she and Herb, his sister, brother-in-law, aunt, and cousin were all coming over. We borrowed a long folding plastic table and folding chairs. I bought extra milk. We spread out the tablecloth that Trent's mother brought and covered the table with deep-fried turkey, oyster stuffing and cranberry salad, and many, many more side dishes that they had brought.

Jean had known I was making stuffing, but brought a large pan of her own anyhow. "We have this every Thanksgiving," she announced. The part of me that is small and mean was irritated.

I don't remember what we talked about over dinner. I do remember how good it felt to have everyone sitting around the long table in Trent's living room and laughing. I also remember that my stuffing disappeared and Jean's didn't, and I was spitefully glad about that.

After the meal was over and the guests had left, Trent was smiling.

"Baby, I did it! I had a meal where my whole family was together and everyone was happy!"

Hunting Season

Every year, Trent assembled his friends to hunt together. This year, most of the usuals appeared: his cousin Steven, his nephews, and a few friends. Out in the barn, pulling on their waders and their hunting coats, Trent told them, "Do not shoot the piebald."

I hadn't gone out that weekend. I like opening day of deer season, when everyone is happy just to be outside and then to come back inside to eat together and usually nobody shoots anything. As the season wears on, though, the mood shifts. It becomes all about the kill. I called Trent after sundown, when the legal hunters come back inside. Trent sounded far away.

"What's wrong?"

"Dick* shot the piebald."

"What?"

"The piebald. He fuckin' shot the piebald."

"But didn't you tell—"

"Hell, yes, I told him. I told them all."

"Oh, Sweet Baby, I'm so sorry."

We were both quiet for a while.

"What did Dick say?"

"He said he couldn't tell it was the piebald, which is bullshit. If you can't tell what you're shooting at . . ."

"Did he at least say he was sorry or something?"

"He said he would have it mounted for me."

A few weeks later, when Trent was hauling the barn's giant trash can out to the road, something caught his eye. He shifted the garbage to get a better look and saw what he suspected and what he did not want to see. Shoved to the bottom was the white head of the piebald.

21. Looking

December 2005

Trent and I decided to look for a place for us to live. His place wasn't selling and mine wasn't yet on the market. Looking wasn't logical—it was an act of hope.

We drove up to northern Michigan to look at a small red cabin on a river. It was so far out of the way that the real estate agent refused to meet us there. The cabin was cute and tidy. We were able to see the inside because it had a snap lock and Trent had a debit card. The house was nice but the real draw was the clear, cold river that ran along the front of the property. You could stand in the living room and throw a rock into it. Trent and I stood on the riverbank, listened to the water, and didn't say much.

Driving back we agreed that Trent could live there but that I couldn't—it was too isolated. The restaurant, the bar, the gas station, and the grocery store were all the same building. Too many residents were missing too many teeth. Even though I attributed that to well water and a lack of fluoride more than a lack of oral hygiene and too much Mountain Dew, it bothered me.

As we drove, we developed our criteria for where we would live. It had to be within two hours of Jenna. It had to be on a river or close to one. It had to be near a town that was big enough to have a library. The house had to be well built.

I napped while Trent took a different route back to Mud Lake. He woke me up as we drove through Newaygo, an old brick town on the Muskegon River. Trent said he had driven through the town as a kid on trips coming back home from being up north and he had always liked it. I liked it, too.

When I got back to Chicago, I went online and looked for real estate near Newaygo. I saw a house that looked promising but it seemed too good to be true and I figured there was something majorly wrong with it. It was probably in a swamp. I pulled out my detailed Michigan map and tried to figure out the defect. I couldn't tell and the Google map was at too small a scale to give any indication. I couldn't even see the house—only the little red Google marker in a sea of trees.

The next night I told Trent about the house and he said we should go check it out.

Friday, December 23, 2005

Christmas 2005 was shaping up to be a hard one. Until this point, Trent and his ex-wife, Doreen,* had made their own adjustment to their custody agreement. The official agreement gave Trent only twenty-four hours on either Christmas Day or Thanksgiving day in alternating years. Doreen and Trent, though, had always split the holiday in half. If Jenna's school was off for twelve days, Trent and Doreen would each take six.

According to the agreement, Trent got Jenna on Thanksgiving Day in odd years and Christmas Day in even years. This year, Doreen decided that Jenna was not going to spend any time with Trent over the Christmas break, but that he could see her if we went to the Christmas gathering at his parents' house. It was custody blackmail.

There was no question about whether we were going. Trent would sit in hell for six hours if it meant he could see his daughter.

We drove to Mud Lake on Friday night, quietly. When we got to the house, we saw the piece of paper taped to the front door. "NOTICE" in large type and underneath that, "FORECLOSURE." It was if we were living a movie script and the director had picked the precise lowest point to bring the hero to his knees.

Neither of us wanted to be in the foreclosed house on Saturday and simply wait for Sunday, Christmas Day, and Jenna. I don't know if it was Trent or if it was me, but one of us proposed driving up to Newaygo the next day to "go look at that house."

Saturday, Christmas Eve 2005

We left late Saturday morning and headed north. The farther north we went, the more snow there was. I had five listings and Trent's detailed Michigan Counties map, so I navigated and Trent drove.

We got to Newaygo and checked out the listings, working from west to east. I ordered the listings in the same way I order the food on my plate—saving what looked like the best for last.

The first four houses were all the same, just with different addresses: modular-construction ranch houses with aluminum siding, much like the Mud Lake house. Trent didn't like them, either. We saw a "For Sale by Owner" sign, not one of the listings, and turned down a road to check it out.

In a small town like Newaygo, not every road gets plowed in the winter. Some do, right away, like M-82. Some get plowed later, and some not at all. Those that don't get plowed are classified as seasonal roads.

The road we turned down had been plowed but the arrow on the next sign directed us to another road that hadn't. The snow wasn't deep but it was packed hard and icy.

Trent cried out, "Boys, them roads are a glare of ice!"— something a father of one of his friends used to say—and eased the car onto it. We got stuck and then unstuck. Whatever house was back there wasn't worth seeing, we decided. If trying to see it once was hard, living there through the winter would be impossible. Trent turned the car around.

We found 76th Street. It had been plowed, up to a point. We drove to where the plowing stopped, at the crest of a tall hill. Just ahead, we could see the "For Sale" sign at the end of a driveway, peeking out between pine trees. We were at eye level with the sign, a steep decline followed by a steep incline between us. We debated how well the Sable would handle the ice. The narrow road at its lowest point ran between a frozen pond to the left and a ditch to the right. If the car went off the road on either side, there would be no getting out without a tow truck.

"What do you think?"

"It doesn't look so bad. What do you think?"

"Might as well find out."

The going was uneventful. Trent eased into the driveway, which had been plowed. The driveway curved between pine trees, then the house came into full view. It was a brown wood house, two stories, with a deep porch. It looked nice.

Trent got out of the car and knocked on the front door. He told the man who answered that we were interested in the house and asked the man if he minded if we walked the property. The man said yes, he did mind, and suggested that Trent get the phone number of the real estate agent from the sign at the bottom of the driveway and call the agent.

Trent called him from the gas station. The agent said he would be happy to show us the house but, because this was Christmas Eve, he wouldn't be able to show it until Tuesday. Tuesday would be fine, we said.

Sunday–Monday, December 25–26, 2005

Doreen changed her mind about Jenna. After the present-opening at Trent's parents' house, she said we could have Jenna that night and the next day. I didn't want to go back to Mud Lake and the foreclosure notice so we went to a bed-and-breakfast in Marshall, Michigan, instead, an old Victorian decorated with evergreens and lights for the holiday.

We were the only ones there so were able to use one end of the long dining room table to play a Monopoly game that spanned two days. The bed-and-breakfast sold commemorative glass Christmas ornaments and Trent bought one so we could be reminded of what a good time we had.

Tuesday, December 27, 2005

We stood on the wide front porch of the brown house in the woods. As Trent knocked on the door, I tried to evaluate the construction: rough-cut cedar board-and-batten siding and, judging by the depth of the windows, 2×6 frame. It looked well made.

The agent opened the door. We were careful to stamp the snow off our boots before we went inside. I was relieved to see that knotty pine was reserved for the east and west walls. North and south walls were drywall, painted white.

Even though the black bear hanging on the fieldstone fireplace vied for my attention, I focused on the house rather than the decor. I ignored the aquamarine sculpted carpet and the incongruous overstuffed floral-print couch and matching armchair.

The house had a nice flow and a two-story great room. The kitchen was open to the dining area and looked back into the woods. The wide porch that ran across the front of the house turned the corner and ran along the side and back as well.

The glass doors in the dining room opened onto the back porch, the backyard, and the woods. At this time of year, the view was mostly white with vertical stripes of brown and green. I could smell pine in the cold air.

I watched Trent stare at the porch and I knew what he was doing. He was counting, calculating the width. He told me later that the porch was eight feet wide and, given that it wrapped three sides of the house, about a hundred feet long. He said that the eight hundred square feet of porch increased the living space by half.

One bedroom and bath were downstairs and another set upstairs. The upstairs loft looked out over the great room and the massive stone fireplace that rose all the way to the peaked ceiling.

We went down to the basement. The walls had no cracks. It didn't feel damp and we could see no indication that it had ever been wet. Trent commented on this and the agent explained that it was almost impossible to have a damp basement in this part of Newaygo; the soil is so sandy the water runs right through it. Trent and I both sighed in relief.

In the Mud Lake house, you can drink the tap water only if you hold your nose. I solved the problem by bringing in bottled water. Trent solved it by drinking beer.

We asked about the water and the agent said that the house had a deep well with a four-inch-diameter pipe for a good supply. Trent then asked about the water quality. The agent explained that the Ice Mountain bottling plant was just a few miles up the road—the water that came out of the faucet would be good enough to bottle and sell.

The agent drew water from the tap and handed the glass to Trent, who took a drink and passed the glass to me. The water was clear and cold. It was and still is the best water I have ever tasted.

We took a walk out back along a narrow path that snaked through the trees. The agent led the way until he ran out of breath and I took over. The snow was deep and the land sloped upward. The agent opted to rest while Trent and I continued.

We turned back after fifteen or twenty minutes because we had learned what we wanted to know: only one other house was visible from the property and you could hardly see it. When the trees had leaves, you wouldn't be able to see it at all.

The agent then showed us another place, a white house, similar in price and style but twice as big and poorly built. We stood in the drafty living room and told the agent that we had seen as much as we wanted to.

We said we'd think about the first house, the brown one. In the car, we determined that it and the detached oversized garage would be perfect. Yes, the garage needed insulation, but Trent could do that even though he hated working with fiberglass. We didn't like the Formica countertops in the kitchen, but those would be easy enough to change out and the cabinets were well made.

We both liked the place so much that we stopped talking about it. Trent's house still needed to sell. Mine wasn't even on the market yet. We drove the rest of the way back to the Mud Lake house in silence.

22. Balance Sheet

Thursday, December 29, 2005

Trent came into the house at Mud Lake to find me sitting at the dining room table with a white legal pad in front of me. I had completed my math exercise and I liked the result. Trent was wary. He remembered what had happened the last time I had sat at this table with a list of figures in front of me. He simply waited for me to talk.

"I've been doing some figuring."

"I can see that."

"Well, you know how we've been thinking that we need to sell your house or my house before we can buy a house for us?"

"Yep."

"Well, I don't think we have to."

"What do you mean?"

"I think I can get another mortgage without selling my house first. Like people do when they buy a vacation house."

Trent didn't say anything so I kept going.

"We could do it backward. I could buy the second home and then sell the first house."

Trent still didn't say anything so I said what I hadn't been saying.

"I think we can buy the brown house."

Trent paused.

"You sure?"

"I have to talk to my mortgage guy to be sure. But I think so."

Trent thought for a moment, looking down. When his face came back up his eyes were bright.

"Well, hell, what are we waiting for!"

Friday, December 30, 2005

I called my lender, John Johnson. He had done the mortgage on my little—six hundred square feet—house in Naperville and on the Chicago two-flat. We talked it through and came up with a strategy. Even though I could carry both houses, I didn't want to. I wanted to sell the Chicago two-flat quickly.

I wasn't that worried about selling the two-flat because by this point I had bought and sold two houses on my own—the

Naperville house and one in Minnesota. I'd sold four houses if you count the two with the man in the purple suspenders, but I'd rather forget about those.

My Minnesota house had sold in one day, at list. The Naperville house had sold in a week for 97 percent of list. The secret to selling a house quickly is accurate pricing, good decorating, and perfectly clean bathrooms. If you mix up pricing with how you feel about your home you will price it too high and waste time. If you really want to move, then price it to sell. I know how to sell a house fast. And for some reason I felt a powerful sense of urgency.

I told Trent that John Johnson said the deal would work. Trent called the real estate agent to schedule time for us to go back and see the brown house again, just to be sure. He was booked on Saturday but said we could see it Sunday, New Year's Day.

Trent called Jenna to see whether she wanted to see it. She did.

Sunday, January 1, 2006

We liked the brown house even more the second time. We did notice, however, that despite the listing saying it had three bedrooms, it had only two. I figured they were counting the loft but since it didn't have a door or a closet, they shouldn't have done.

Jenna wanted to know which bedroom would be hers when she visited. Trent told her it would be the downstairs one. We both tried not to react to the idea of Jenna's visiting. She had come to Mud Lake or Chicago every other weekend in 2004, but that had pretty much stopped in 2005. Jenna had

144

then said that she didn't want to see her father anymore. Doreen said she didn't have to. I had wasted my time drawing up visitation schedules and giving them to Trent to give to Doreen. Trent had wasted his time at the lawyer's office.

The lawyer told Trent that since Jenna was almost thirteen, if she didn't want to see her father, she didn't have to. Trent pushed his case with Doreen but all she said was, "Jenna doesn't want to see you and I'm not going to make her." So, as we walked around the brown house with Jenna, Trent tried not to get his hopes up.

We had agreed that we would look only at the brown house with Jenna. Trent surprised me when he asked her if she wanted to see the white house down the road. I thought this was unwise but said nothing. I didn't understand then, but all he wanted was more time. More time with his daughter. More seconds, more minutes, more of a chance. Other than the Thanksgiving dinner and the two days at Christmas, he hadn't seen her in six months or more and wasn't ready to start the drive back to Battle Creek. Not yet.

Jenna liked the white house better. She didn't see the poor construction. She saw soaring ceilings and four bedrooms. Maybe she saw parties with her friends. Trent explained that the white house would use more propane in one month than the brown house would use in three. Jenna was unmoved. In the car, Jenna started pleading to buy the white house instead. I said nothing for several minutes. Then I spoke up, wondering if I would regret it later.

"Trent, does Jenna have a vote?"

"What?"

"In the decision about which house we buy, does Jenna have a vote?"

"No. She doesn't. You and I have a vote."

"Then why did you even bring me up here?" Jenna wailed.

"I wanted you to see where we're going to live."

Jenna put in her earbuds, tucked her head down, and listened to her music. Trent and I were quiet for a while and then started talking softly about the brown house.

January 2–3, 2006

On Monday we made an offer. Trent is a better negotiator than I, but in this case neither of us was very good. The problem was that we weren't willing to walk away, and if you're not willing to walk, you've given away your negotiating power. On Tuesday we agreed to a price—only $1,000 less than list.

We wandered around looking at snack food and soda bottles in a convenience store, waiting for the faxed confirmation to come through. When it did, Trent turned to me.

"Congratulations, Sweet Baby, you just bought a house for your birthday!"

He was right. It was my birthday. I had almost forgotten.

We went back to Mud Lake and celebrated the brown house in Newaygo and me.

23. I Did It

January–February 2006

After I signed the contract but before we moved in, Trent's night kicking got worse. It had subsided over the last year but suddenly it and the nightmares were back every night. One night, he hit me hard in the shin. I moved to the bed in the other room. He woke me another night. But this time, instead of being on his side and kicking off the bed, he was on his back and kicking both legs into the air. And he was talking.

"I did it. I did it. I did it. I did it."

At first I thought he was talking in his sleep, which he had done sometimes when he had nightmares. But he was awake, with his eyes squeezed shut and tears coming out the corners.

"You did what?"

"I did it."

"What did you do?"

"I did it."

"What?"

Trent clenched his right fist and drew it, thumb down, across his abdomen. I could imagine the long-bladed knife he had held years earlier.

"You cut yourself?"

"I did it."

"With a knife?"

"Yeah."

"Because you wanted your parents to come and tell you they were wrong and they loved you."

"Yeah."

"But they didn't come. And you knew they weren't going to."

"No . . . they wouldn't."

"What happened?"

"I drove myself to the hospital. The doctors knew I did it. They said, 'You did this,' but I said, 'No, I was in a fight. A bar fight.' They knew I was lying but I wasn't going to tell them. They would just put me away. They knew but I didn't tell them. They stitched me up and let me go."

I held him and we both cried. We cried for a long time.

A Bullet

Saturday morning and we were at Mud Lake. I was sitting at the dining room table, having cereal for breakfast. Trent was outside, saying good-bye to Dick, who had visited the day before and stayed the night.

Even before he killed the piebald, I had never liked Dick, at first simply because he borrowed Trent's things and returned them broken, without apology or offer of compensation. After Trent told me a few stories about him, I liked him even less.

The dining room table was lit up with sunlight through the window and I was feeling happy. Dick was leaving, which was good; Trent and I had found the house in Newaygo, which was good; and it seemed that we would soon be living in the same place, which would be very good.

I finished my cereal and relaxed in the captain's chair. My heart lifted and mingled with the sunlight in the room. I rested my head on the back of the chair and smiled. And then something on the ceiling—a glint—caught my eye. My mouth went dry, my skin felt cold. I stood up and looked at the glint but wasn't positive it was what I thought it might be. I stood on the captain's chair closest to the object to get a closer look.

What had glinted was sunk into the drywall but enough was showing to identify it. A bullet. It wasn't a big bullet like you see on television or in the movies. It was small and golden, almost elegant.

I sat back down in my chair but felt as if I was falling. My stomach rolled. I thought about Trent's headaches and nightmares and the kicking, which had been bad for weeks. I thought about a man who treated me so sweetly but who had so little regard for himself.

Trent came inside and with a "Good morning, Sweet Baby" sat down in the chair I had just stood on. I had my question ready but wasn't ready for wherever it might take us.

"How did the bullet get in the ceiling?"

The question wiped the smile from his face. He looked at me, weighing either my ability to hear what he had to say or his ability to say it.

"A gun put it there."

"How did a gun put it there?"

"I shot it there."

"Why did you shoot the ceiling?"

"Because Dick convinced me to shoot the ceiling instead."

My stomach rolled again.

"What were you going to shoot?"

Trent didn't answer right away. I waited.

"Last night, Dick and I were sitting here. I said that I didn't know if God wanted me alive or dead. So I put a bullet in the gun, spun the chamber, and put the gun to my head. I said that if I shot the gun and I was still alive then God wanted me alive. But if I shot the gun and I died, then God wanted me dead. Dick said I didn't have to die to find out if God wanted me dead. Dick said I could just shoot the gun and if it fired a bullet, I would know that God wanted me dead."

Trent looked up at the ceiling.

"There's the bullet. So God wants me dead."

He looked stricken as he said it.

I countered, "Or you could say that God put Dick here to convince you to shoot the ceiling instead and God wants you alive."

"There's a bullet in the ceiling. Proof. God wants me dead."

"That's not how I see it. If God wanted you dead, you'd be dead already. As long as you're living, God wants you alive."

Trent said nothing more. I didn't know what else to say. I got up from my chair, fit myself into his lap, wrapped my arms around him and wondered if we would ever make it to Newaygo.

Split Open

I don't know how someone takes an eight-inch hunting knife to his own abdomen and stabs himself fifteen or twenty times. I do, however, have a pretty good idea of what it would look like.

The man in the purple suspenders ate pasta almost every night. His favorite was linguini with clam sauce. He was a very good cook. One night he had bad stomach pains. He looked yellow. I said I should take him to the hospital. He said not to, he was going to be fine.

I thought about not taking him and letting him die because I was pretty sure something was very wrong with him, not because of the pains but because of the yellow. Even his eyes looked yellow. I decided that I didn't want to feel guilty if he died so I took him to the emergency room.

"Pasta is Elmer's glue for the intestines," the doctor said. The man in the purple suspenders' intestines had gotten stuck together. The food he ate couldn't pass through. It jammed up until his intestines burst. That is what made him yellow. The doctor said if I hadn't brought the man to the ER, he would have been dead in four hours.

The doctor said that he needed surgery but the man in the purple suspenders wanted to wait until the morning. The doctor said, "No. We have to do it now," and called the surgeon.

My job was going to be wound care so right away the nurses started teaching me how to change the dressing. Eight pieces of gauze had to be soaked in saline and then placed in the man's belly, which looked like a giant cantaloupe with a slice missing. The nurses told me that I would need less gauze as the wound healed.

When the nurses were gone, the man in the purple suspenders asked me what it looked like, this wound in his body. I told him that just under the skin was a thick layer of yellow fat that looked like chicken fat only not as shiny. At the bottom, where the two sides of the missing slice came together, were stitches holding his abdominal muscles together.

The day he was to be discharged the man in the purple suspenders told me I was wrong, that there wasn't yellow fat under his skin, it was pink flesh. I didn't say anything.

I wanted to say, "You stupid idiot. It's fat and the reason it looks pink rather than yellow is because your body has already started vascularizing it so it can heal. You can thank me for changing your dressing and you can thank me for taking to the ER because I was tempted to just let you die."

So this is what I thought about as I held Trent. I thought about how his abdominal muscles would have contracted as he stabbed himself. The blade would have sliced through his skin and his fat but wouldn't have gone very deeply into his muscle.

I wondered what his abdomen must have looked like, crisscrossed with stab wounds. I wondered how many stitches it had taken to sew all those slashes back together. I wondered about the places where his scars joined and made triangles, and if the stitches were the only thing that had kept those pieces from falling out.

24. Coming Home

Friday, March 24, 2006

In February, the two-flat went on the market and sold in two days at list price, for 9.7 percent more than I had paid three years earlier. We then closed on the brown house in Newaygo and set the move-in date for March 1st, though because of work I would stay in the two-flat until March 25th. Trent moved in immediately. The Mud Lake house was still both for sale and up for foreclosure auction.

Finally, it was time for me to go. The last thing I did before leaving work was call Trent to say that I would be there around eleven that night. He reminded me about the road being blocked with the flooding and said that he would leave a canoe out so I could get across. He told me to be sure to have my flashlight handy and to remember how dark the country is at night. I had forgotten about the flooding.

The winter had been strange in Newaygo. It had stormed a week or so earlier. What normally would have been snow had been ten to twelve inches of rain. Because the ground was frozen, the rain had nowhere to go. It filled the low parts in the land to make lakes that rose and spilled over roads and kept rising.

Earlier that day, Trent had paddled the new lake that straddled the road, checking it out. He had dipped his four-foot canoe paddle down into the water but couldn't touch bottom.

Only five homes are on the dirt road to the house in Newaygo and all are on the south side of it: the manufactured home, the trailer, the ranch house with the straight driveway, the big house with the curving driveway, and the brown house (now ours). The road runs level until you get to the driveway to the big house, where it takes a sharp dip. Then it comes back up again to get to our driveway. The big dip between the neighbor's house and ours was where the rain had made a lake.

On the drive to Newaygo, the roads started out wet but switched to white packed snow on the last road to our house. It wasn't too slippery. At the crest of the hill by the neighbor's house, I slowed, not sure where the lake would start.

It was close. The road was narrow so I pulled my car as far off the road as I could, up against the embankment that rose off to the right. The canoe was waiting, shiny silver in my headlights. I grabbed the flashlight and turned off my car. Without the light from the headlights, I couldn't see the lake or the canoe or the switch on the flashlight. I opened the car door to trigger the dome light, then turned on the flashlight and got out of the car. The air was cold and damp.

I left everything in the car—the boxes from work, the boxes from the house in Chicago that held everything I needed for my last week in the city, after the movers had taken everything else. I had slept on the inflatable bed borrowed from Trent's camping supplies.

I didn't want to paddle across the lake in the skinny canoe in the dark. If I fell out, it would be cold, and if I couldn't touch the bottom, my clothes would make it hard to swim across. I thought about walking around the lake but it was big and I would be walking through the woods in the dark. I decided paddling across was the better of two poor options.

After moving the front of the canoe into the water, I took the paddle out from under the seat, got into the canoe, and pushed off. It was quiet and cold and dark. I couldn't see the car I had left and could barely see the light from our house through the trees. I spoke aloud to myself.

"Jule, what have you done?"

I don't remember any more of that night, only waking up the next morning. Trent was looking at me, smiling. Because he didn't speak, I did.

"Good morning, Sweet Baby."

Trent's smile stretched even further. "You're here. You're really here."

"You didn't think I would come?"

"Unh-uh."

It made me a little sad because I realized he was telling the truth—he really thought I wouldn't come. That realization made me understand why, once he had moved in, he didn't leave until I got there. He was using himself as bait.

"I'm here, Sweet Baby, I'm really here."

Trent laughed and grabbed me and hugged me.

"If you wanted to leave, you'd have to paddle your way out!"

Trent explained his theory of why the road to our house had flooded. Paving the road that led to the road to our house had changed the drainage. He told me how he had walked the woods to track where the water had come from. He had tracked through the woods until he came out the other side, at a farm, where the flow of the water had uprooted the frozen cornstalks.

We stayed in bed for a long time, talking and smiling. We were together and we were home.

TOGETHER

25. Newaygo Mantra

April 2006

It was in our bedroom in Newaygo where Trent and I started saying two sentences that became our mantra.

We only said it when we were in bed, lying on our backs, Trent with his hands either behind his head or one arm down by his side. If his right hand was down by his side, then my left hand was resting in his cupped palm. My left little, fourth, and middle toes were touching the top rounded part of Trent's ankle.

"We're going to love each other forever," Trent would say.

And I would respond, "Sometimes I think we got born just so we could touch each other."

I don't know if you can really love someone forever or if you can be born just to touch someone. But I also don't know that you can't.

We both experienced some culture shock when we first got to Newaygo. His was at the RadioShack, where he had gone to figure out why we were getting only one television channel.

"What's it take to get TV reception around here?"

"An antenna!"

"I got one. But I'm only getting one channel."

"Huh. You should be getting two."

When Trent got back home, he realized that we were indeed getting both channels—it was just hard to tell because they were showing the same programming.

My culture shock came at the bank, the second time I walked in. All three tellers greeted me by name. I had been banking at Citibank for twenty years and not one person there knew me. Trent and I would have no secrets at the bank in Newaygo. We started keeping notes of the things that we found amusing, frustrating, or just plain weird.

Getting directions: "Excuse me, do you know where the library is?"

"Yep, right across from where the hotel burned down."

"Oh no. When did it burn?"

"1962."

At the courthouse, from a fellow citizen: "My neighbor owe me 500 dollar because his dawg ate my goat but he ain' payin' it and the judge said my goat's worth 500 dollar. He got to pay me my 500 dollar."

At the courthouse, from a police officer (in reference to someone they had put in jail the night before): "Couldn't put him in the car. Too big. Had to go get the van and put him in the back."

On a sign in a front yard:

BUNNIES FOR SALE

$8 Living, $10 Dead

On a paper plate tacked to a cork board (in a store that sold beer, pizza, gas, ammo, ice cream, and bait):
>KAR 4 SALE IT RUN GOOD WHEN YOU JUMP IT

We had gotten ourselves to Newaygo, a strange and wonderful place. But we couldn't rest yet. We still had to sell the house in Mud Lake or watch it slip away in foreclosure. The wheels were turning on both at the same time.

26. Ashes

April–May 2006

The house at Mud Lake went up for auction. There were no bidders. The next day, Trent's real estate agent called. Someone had made an offer on the house.

Trent initially wanted to turn it down because he thought it was too low. Elaine had warned me about this. She had said that a part of Trent believed he didn't deserve good. In some ways he would prefer familiar misery to unfamiliar good.

I pointed out that it was the only offer, that the house was in foreclosure, that the offer would cover the mortgage and then some. His choice was to accept the offer or lose the house and walk away with nothing but a debt. I reminded him that whether he accepted the offer or not, either way he was losing the house.

The closing was set for Friday, May 5th. The requirement to close was that the house and barn be clean and empty by noon, Saturday, May 6th.

When Trent and Doreen had bought the house in 1991, it had been full. Trent called the previous owners pack rats. Today we tend to call them hoarders. Trent cleaned out the front of the barn, where the cement floor was, but never entirely emptied the back of the barn.

Both of us knew how difficult it would be to meet the closing condition. I no longer thought of the house at Mud Lake as a building of wood and stone. I thought of it as a spiteful ex-lover who would rather have us dead than gone.

Trent got to work. He spent April at Mud Lake, not Newaygo. I came on the weekends except for the last week, when I came on Wednesday. I heard Trent telephone Dick.

"I told you years ago to get your boat out of my barn. Get it now or I'm selling it."

This was Dick's 28-foot motorboat. He kept it in Trent's barn because it was free storage. Dick came and got it. As we worked, we sorted things into three piles: Newaygo, garage sale, and trash. Every now and then I would find something to put in the Newaygo pile. When I found four wool blankets, folded and musty on an old wooden table at the back of the barn where the floor was dirt, I asked Trent where they had come from. When he said they were O.T.'s, I didn't put them on the Newaygo pile but in the back of my car to keep them safe.

The garage sale went well because Trent had the right attitude and strategy—price it to sell it. We both knew that anything unsold would have to be trashed. The fiberglass ice-fishing house with the canvas cover went for $100.

The trash items that could be burned went into the burn pile, a hole in the ground the size of a quarter of a football field. For days we carried things out of the barn to the burn pile until the hole was filled. Then it became a hill.

On Friday afternoon, May 5th, we went to the closing, filthy. When we got back to Mud Lake, Trent poured gasoline on the burn pile. Then we went back to work, hauling more dusty things out of the barn. That night, Trent shoved some burning cardboard into the pile in various locations, as he told me that usually when he lit a burn pile he did it with flaming arrows. The fire started slowly, with small flames where the cardboard had been placed.

"What will we do if it doesn't burn?"

Trent kept his eyes on the spots of flame. "It'll burn."

We watched it for a few minutes. Not much seemed to be happening. A couple spots of flame looked a little bigger, maybe. Suddenly the entire pile burst into flame. It was so bright and so hot that we had to step back. It got even hotter, the flames went even higher into the night sky. I looked at the fire and I looked at the barn, maybe twenty yards away.

"Will the barn be okay?"

"Should be. She's done this before."

I went back inside the house to finish cleaning the kitchen. Even though it was going to be gutted, I didn't want to give the buyers any reason to walk away when they did their closing inspection. Trent came back in the house.

"Sweet Baby, you've never seen me ride. I want you to see how I can climb trees."

I went outside and stood on the back stoop.

Trees lined the border between the backyard grass and the swamp. The moon must have been full, because I could see the trees behind the smoke.

The headlight of the three-wheeler came out of the barn and cut through the smoke. Trent was a black shadow backlit by fog and fire.

He drove the three-wheeler up the trunk of a tree until he was about four or five feet off the ground, then rolled back to tackle another tree. It was a beautiful melding of man and machine, and for the first time I understood why he loved it. He wasn't just climbing trees. He was dancing. I watched him until the headlight turned away and he disappeared into the swamp.

May 5, 2006

After finishing scrubbing the kitchen, spending too much time on the worn pine cabinets, I ran a sponge over both bathrooms. Then I fell into bed. I woke up in the night, the bright numbers of the digital clock showing that it was after three o'clock. Trent was not beside me.

Wandering out to the dining room, I could see Trent on the other side of the window, tending a fire. He wasn't tending the burn pile. That one had burned up quickly. This was a different one. It wasn't back by the barn but in the backyard, on the grass. It was small, about the size of a keg of beer. Trent had a long pole he rested on except when he lifted it to stir the fire.

The outside air was cooler than it had been earlier. I stood next to Trent and felt him wobble from exhaustion.

"Let me do this for a while."

"I got it."

"You look like you're ready to fall over. I've at least had some sleep. I'll do it."

He leaned the long pole toward me and I took it. He said, "Keep turning it, so it burns," then turned back to the house. I turned to the fire.

It was a quiet night. The fog had cleared and I watched the thin line of smoke curl up toward the stars. A car stopped on the road in front of the house. I didn't know if it was a police car or a curious neighbor. I ran the pole through the fire and stood tall, as if I knew what I was doing. Minutes later, when I looked back toward the road, the car was still there. Many more minutes later, it was gone.

I stirred the fire until the dark sky turned to early pale and all that was left was ashes.

May 6, 2006

My car and Trent's truck were loaded with whatever was left that we were taking to Newaygo. Everything else had been taken, sold, or burned.

I wanted to leave and go to Newaygo but Trent wanted to stay and hand the keys to the new owners. I was too tired to disagree. The new owners were either tardy or allowed extra time to be sure we were gone. Instead of noon, they came at one fifteen. The buyers were a young couple. Both sets of parents were with them. Trent offered them a beer. The young couple, to be polite, accepted. The parents declined, then one of the fathers changed his mind and said he'd have one. The arm that distributed the beers was dirty, as was the rest of him. Both of us, our clothes and our skins, were blotched with sweat and soot. Trent's hair looked brown.

A few swigs of beer were drunk and Trent handed over the keys. Then one of the fathers, the one without the beer, spoke.

"You can go now."

Trent laughed and the father said it again. "You can go now."

I took Trent's arm and walked us to our vehicles.

When we got to Newaygo, Trent took the downstairs shower and I took the one upstairs, making the pleasant discovery that the hot water heater could handle both at once.

It was midafternoon but we went straight to bed and slept the dead sleep of the exhausted. I slept for twenty-one hours, Trent for twenty-four.

27. Tamarack Creek

May 2006

At the closing for the Mud Lake house, one of the line items to be paid by the seller was a fee to the mortgage company to remove the house from foreclosure. This fee was in addition to the back payments owed that were also to be paid by the seller. The fee reduced what Trent walked away with by half.

After we woke, Trent said he wanted to go shopping. He wanted to buy kayaks. I understood. I had done something similar in college, after some stock that my grandmother had given me fell to the point that what had been worth several thousand dollars was worth three hundred. I sold the stock and bought a guitar. We bought four kayaks (two for us, two for other people we might go kayaking with), four life vests, four paddles, and two wetbags.

At the store, Trent told the salesperson that we had been kayaking on the Muskegon and wanted to try something new—what about Tamarack Creek? She said she had never kayaked Tamarack but others had, there should be enough water this time of year, and it would be cold if we fell out but it should be fine.

She was wrong.

Alarms have always gone off in my head about situations and people and places but I have trained myself to ignore them. I tell myself everything is normal, I am fine, everything will be okay.

I stayed on Tamarack Creek even though the alarms were ringing.

The plan was to get to the creek by eight in the morning because Trent and the person at the kayak store had calculated that the trip would take eight hours. We were late. This was our first time putting the Yakima rack on the Jeep that we had gotten to replace the Sable, and putting the kayaks on the rack, and gathering all our gear. We didn't pull off M-82 onto the dirt road that led to the put-in point until about nine.

Whenever I go on adventures, I keep a dual-column account in my head, a list of things working for or against me. Today, being an hour behind the planned start time was a check mark on the negative side. But the day was sunny and warm and we were both feeling good. I put a check mark on the positive side and figured we were even.

Trent and I each had canoeing experience. Mine was minor, a few backpacking or canoeing trips in the Boundary Waters of Minnesota and Canada. Trent's was extensive, canoeing the Kalamazoo and all over Mud Lake and the streams that run in and out of it. We had both kayaked only twice.

I had lobbied with Trent that our first trip in our new kayaks not be on water we'd never been on before, but I didn't push it. Trent wanted a fresh experience on the Tamarack and I went along with it. I figured that the worst that could happen is we would both get wet.

Of the four kayaks we had bought, two were long (fourteen feet) and two were short (eleven feet). We decided we'd use the longs on the Muskegon and the shorts on smaller rivers where we'd need better maneuverability. We brought the shorts to the Tamarack.

We put on our life vests—mine was bright yellow, Trent's was khaki. As we slid the kayaks into the water, Trent reminded me that kayaks are unsteady and to be sure to step into the middle of the kayak when I got in. The narrow creek ran between steep wooded banks. The previous winter had seen lots of snow, which had been followed that spring by a lot of rain. The water was high and fast and cold.

I got into my kayak ungracefully but successfully and was pleased. Waiting for Trent to get into his kayak, I held on to a branch on the bank to stay in place. I heard something behind me and carefully turned to see Trent hauling his kayak back up the bank. He was wet. I put a mark in the negative column. The tally was no longer even.

We kayaked the short distance from the put-in point to under the overpass for M-82. The level ground under the overpass was a popular place for fishermen, but no one was fishing that morning. The sun came through the leaves in dappled light. The air was fresh.

Deadfalls

A deadfall is a tree that has died and fallen across the water, partially or completely obstructing progress down the river. We soon came to our first, a large one stretching from one bank to the other, with too little clearance to kayak underneath. We angled our kayaks to one side of the creek, pulled them out, hauled them down the bank past the deadfall, and put them back in the water.

Each of the kayaks weighed fifty-one pounds, the paddles were two pounds or so, the wetbags a few more pounds. Water in a kayak added eight pounds per gallon.

The creek makes sharp turns as it flows to Croton Dam Pond, lurching from right to left like a drunk in a narrow alley. The turns meant that we could never see farther ahead than ten yards, twenty if we were lucky. We came around a turn to see a huge deadfall, but with clearance at one side. We paddled to the clearance, folded ourselves forward in our kayaks, and let the water carry us under and beyond the tree. The next one came fast. Trent paddled quickly to get ahead of me. He said we could clear it underneath, but not by folding forward, because our backs would get scratched. He said we would need to scooch down in our kayaks, face up like a kid in a bathtub. I scooched as low as I could go and then watched the bark pass inches from my face.

Sitting up, we saw both that the creek straightened out and a series of deadfalls. These were smaller trees with lots of branches that denied passage. The right bank was steep rock so we paddled to the left. Once again we pulled our kayaks out of the water, hauled them through brush, and put them back in the creek.

My accounting was recording more checks in the negative column. Each deadfall, for example. I decided to award us one in the positive column for getting so good at getting our kayaks out of the water and then back in again.

We paddled through an open stretch of water and saw a man standing in his backyard. He had probably come down to the creek to see what was making all the noise. He called out to us.

"Where you headed?"

"Croton Pond."

"Oh."

"Think it's about eight hours?"

"Maybe twelve."

Four check marks in the negative, one for every extra hour. I looked ahead, saw more deadfalls, and decided it was time to stop the accounting. This trip wasn't fun. It was work and I needed to concentrate.

Slammed

I was feeling pretty good about our navigating. Some of the deadfalls came part way into the narrow creek and we could paddle around them. Some had enough clearance for us to go under. The rest we portaged around. At this point, I was worried about three things: water, exhaustion, and darkness.

We were expending a lot of energy paddling and portaging around deadfalls.

We would need food, which we had enough of, and water, which we didn't. Since our trip length had increased by half, I wasn't sure we were physically up to the challenge. And since the trip was now estimated to take twelve hours and it was about ten o'clock in the morning, we would be kayaking the last four hours in the dark. I didn't know if that was even possible.

The world was very small. It included a creek, a steep bank on one side and woods all around, two people in two kayaks, and at least one of whom didn't know what to do. I decided to think about what to do after the next deadfall, which was coming up fast.

The tree was larger than some but not huge. The trunk was maybe the size of a telephone pole and dipped into the water on the left side. It looked as if there was enough room between where the tree met the water and the bank to paddle around. I angled my kayak to the left, but the rocks made strange eddies that grabbed the back end of my kayak and turned me 90 degrees. I couldn't get the kayak back in line even though I was paddling as hard as I could. It was being pulled sideways to the deadfall.

The kayak hit the deadfall hard but it and I were both okay. When you're kayaking you don't realize how quickly the water is moving. When you're stopped and the water is punching your kayak against a deadfall, you realize that it is a lot faster than you thought. I was stuck.

If I tried to get out of the kayak on the high side, where the water was coming from, the water would slam me into the kayak. The only option was to climb out on the tree side. I got my arms curled around the top of the tree, but as I started to pull myself out, the reduced weight in the boat allowed the water to grab my kayak and flip it. The top half of my body was curled around the tree, the bottom half was in the water, the creek was pounding my kayak into my back, and the water was pulling at my legs.

It took everything I had just to hang on to the tree. I've always had strong legs but weaker upper body strength. I tried to pull myself out of the water onto the tree but it was like trying to do a pull-up with a weightlifter hanging from my legs. Somehow the water pulled the kayak away and I saw the little beige boat slip ahead of me and get caught in the next deadfall. It felt good not to have the kayak pounding my back anymore, but I still had a problem.

I wasn't going to be able to pull myself up. I was going to have to let go of the tree, push myself down into the water, let the water take me under, and then swim up to the surface. If I waited too long to let go, I would be too exhausted to come up for air. If I didn't push down hard enough, the life vest would keep me afloat and the river would pummel my head into the tree trunk. I hoped there weren't any branches under the tree that might hang me up and keep me under longer than I could stay there. I was just getting ready to let go when Trent spoke.

"Stay there."

He was on the rock ledge to my right and he was stepping out onto the tree. I didn't watch, partly because it was too hard to turn my head and partly because I didn't want to think about how narrow the tree was or what would happen if he fell off. I hung on until I felt Trent's hands grab my shoulders, pull me up, and drag me back to the rock ledge. We stood there, backs flat against the rock, catching our breath, looking at the water. We both now knew that getting wet wasn't the worst that could happen.

Under

Other people would have decided to call it quits. I was wet, I was cold, I was tired. My arms ached from hanging on to the tree, my back hurt from being pummeled by a kayak. But I didn't want to be the reason we stopped the adventure.

We eased ourselves into the water downstream of the deadfall that had nearly done me in and swam to our kayaks. As I paddled, I noticed that my wetbag was missing from the front of the kayak. The four buckles were still there but the bag was gone. The water had ripped it away.

We approached another deadfall with whitewater swirling around it. This time I was determined not to get slammed into a tree. As the creek grabbed the back of my kayak and spun it around, I readied myself. When the kayak got within a few feet of the deadfall, I slipped out of the boat and into the swirling water. I dove under, swam a few strokes, then popped out on the other side of the deadfall. I called back to Trent.

"Go under. It's easier."

When I turned back toward Trent, he was sliding out of his boat and into the water. I waited for him to pop up but he didn't. It seemed to take longer than it should have. He finally came up, close to me. His face was red with blood and he couldn't see. I grabbed his arm and led him to the bank and pulled him toward a small ledge. I left him there and rescued our kayaks. When I got back, Trent had taken off his T-shirt and was wiping his face with it. Luckily, the gash was across his eyebrow and not anyplace worse. He sat on the ledge and I stood, surveying our situation. The banks on either side of the creek were steep rock; we wouldn't be able to walk out. There was no option but to go back into the water.

Out

We paddled around a couple of small deadfalls, then spotted a patch of land next to a low rise of earth. It was the landing point to the backyard of a beautiful house and a perfect spot to get out. I landed my kayak and got out, waiting for Trent to join me. He pulled up alongside the bank but didn't get out of his kayak.

"I think we should get out here," I said.

"Why?"

"Because you're bleeding."

"I'm fine."

"You might be fine but I'm not. I want to get out here."

"But we're going to Croton."

I looked at the blood coming through the T-shirt tied around his head and realized that the wound may have damaged more than just flesh.

"We're not going to Croton. We're not going to make it."

"We can make it."

"It going to get dark, Trent. It's already after noon and we're not even halfway there."

"I think we can make it."

"If you go, you're going alone. I'm getting out here."

This was the first time he appeared to consider my proposal.

"But we don't know where we are."

"We don't. But we know that M-82 is south of here and south is that way."

I gestured toward the sun, then reached down and pulled my kayak to the higher ground of the trimmed backyard. Trent followed. We walked across the backyard, up the driveway, dropped the kayaks, and walked out onto the street and turned south, which was left. We walked past several houses until we came to one that advertised child care. I knocked on the door and begged a ride back to the Jeep.

Money is hard to come by in Newaygo. I gave the woman $20 for her trouble and for gas. When I got back to Trent, he was wandering in the street. Once we got back to the Jeep, I took him to the emergency room, where they took an X-ray of his head and cleaned and stitched his wound. The doctor said that everybody thinks river water is clean but it isn't. Looking straight at me he said that if something like this ever happened again, I should immediately rinse the wound with clean water. He must have sensed that Trent was prone to injury.

We never kayaked on Tamarack Creek again, and every time we drove on M-82 where the bridge crosses the creek, Trent would say, "Tamar-ak-ak-ak-ak-ak-ak."

28. Mother's Day

May 14, 2006

Trent and I had gone to bed and were lying quietly side by
side when Trent noticed that I was crying.

"What's wrong, Sweet Baby?"

"I never had any babies."

A long pause.

"Do you want us to have a baby, Sweet Baby?"

"No, I'm too old. But just because I don't want one doesn't
mean I can't be sad that I never had one."

Trent laid his arm across my chest. A few more tears came
out the corners of my eyes.

"I think I would have been a good mom."

"You're a great mom, Sweet Baby! You're a mom to
Jenna."

"I'm not her real mom."

"You're as real as the one she's got."

Ginger

Trent came into the house, palm out and up. At first I thought
he might have cut himself, but it wasn't blood in his palm, it
was a small turtle. This one was bigger than Ernest was when
he had crawled into the Mud Lake garage, but not by much,
and it didn't have Ernest's bright-orange stripes but was all
dark green. We had a brief debate about putting it in the tank
with Ernest. Trent said the tank wasn't any more dangerous
than the outside world, opened the top, and lowered his
palm into the green water. The turtle swam off immediately.
Ernest plopped off his rock to swim over and check out his

new neighbor, then swam away. We named her Ginger, and I took this new life in a hard shell as a good omen.

Construction

Trent spent May insulating and putting up OSB sheathing, a specialized engineered particleboard that is stronger and cheaper than plywood, on the inside of the garage. He added insulation to make the garage warmer in the winter and cooler in the summer and put up the OSB to stiffen the walls and make the garage sturdier.

In June, he built me an office in a corner of the basement. When he was sketching the plans, he asked if I was going to be okay working in a room without windows. I laughed and explained that I had been working without windows for most of my career, that only twice did I have an office with a window by my desk. He was aghast.

He then decided to put in a stained-glass window, not on the wall with the door but on the wall to my left as I sat at the desk, the wall that would separate the office from the twin beds on the other side.

October 2006

I had started a corporate training consulting business in July and was subcontracting for Robin, another consultant. After completing a few small projects for her, she graduated me to a larger one. It was a big project for an important client and it would take both of us working full time to complete it.

One day, which was quickly turning into night, something had gone wrong. Either she had miscommunicated with me or I had misunderstood. Either way, the document she received from me that morning had fallen short of expectations and I was reworking it.

At about six in the evening, Trent brought me dinner, and at about nine or ten he brought me a little plate of cheese and crackers. He had made a smiley face on each cracker. At about eleven, he asked whether I would be coming to bed soon. I realized that I wasn't. I had underestimated how much time the rework would take. I told him I needed several more hours. We were both disappointed.

I thought he would just go to bed but I heard some noise on the other side of the wall. After a few minutes of clanking, sudden brightness. The stained-glass window was lit as if it were above ground and the sun was shining through.

Trent poked his head back in the office. "You might have to be up all night but it doesn't have to feel like it."

He had taken his 500-watt construction lamp and set it up between the twin beds, facing the stained glass, shining into the office. He was right. I worked all night but it didn't feel like it. Just before seven the next morning, I sent the document to Robin. It was good and I went to bed, smiling.

Maybe Trent couldn't rotate the Earth, but he could make it feel that he could.

29. Christmas in Newaygo

Christmas Eve 2006

In 2006, we were scheduled to have Jenna for Christmas. I told Trent that he could go see his parents if he wanted but I wasn't leaving our house. He said he wasn't, either, that we were going to have a family Christmas. If his parents wanted to see us, they could come to Newaygo.

When he told his mother our plans, she was again angry and again accused him of being selfish and breaking the family tradition. He said it was time for new traditions and that she could come here. He was old enough, he explained, to have his own Christmas in his own house.

On Christmas Eve day, after picking up Jenna at the rendezvous site, we stopped at a tree farm. Jenna was wearing slippers and the snow was deep, so I gave her the big boots I kept in the back of the Jeep. She and Trent picked out the biggest, widest tree that would fit in the spot we had planned for it—up in the loft, outside our bedroom, looking over the living room.

Late that afternoon, I made a raspberry pie, Trent's favorite, something special for dessert. I asked Jenna whether she wanted to design the top, which she did. The top pie crust needed at least a few holes to vent the steam.

Jenna picked up the paring knife and bent over the naked crust and carved a large heart with "JTJ" in the middle of it. She smiled.

"Jenna, Trent, Jule. JTJ."

We usually opened gifts on Christmas Day, but Trent wanted us to open a few small ones on Christmas Eve. Trent had one for each of us, including Ernest and Ginger. Inside the packages were wooden ornaments. Each of us had a different animal (Trent's was a deer) and each had our names carved into the top.

He gave me an extra one—a photograph of the house, etched into acrylic, with "HOME SWEET HOME" across the top. It was of course my favorite.

After the ornaments were in the tree, Jenna showed us how to form a star with our fingers by each person making a V with their index and middle fingers, and then putting our fingertips together. The star required the V from both of Jenna's hands and both of Trent's but only one of mine (it was a five-pointed star). With my free hand, I took a photo of our hand-star, the lights from the tree shining behind it.

Christmas Day 2006

On Christmas morning, we opened presents, after which Trent made banana pancakes. I don't remember any of the presents except the fleece socks I got for all of us—extra-large camouflage for Trent, large blue with snowflakes for me, and medium pink and orange paisley for Jenna.

We lay in front of the fireplace and propped our feet up on the hearth and took pictures of our newly socked feet. Trent's feet were in the middle, Jenna's and mine were on either side, just like the letters on the pie crust. Then we interwove our feet and took more pictures.

At two in the afternoon, Doreen called. She wanted to come get Jenna because Jenna's sister was going to be proposed to that night and she wanted Jenna to be there. She said she would be in Newaygo to pick Jenna up at four. Trent and Doreen's conversation escalated. Trent's main point was that it was Christmas Day and that, according to the custody agreement, he had Jenna for all of it.

Rather than just stand there and feel helpless, I went upstairs to the file cabinet and pulled out the Jenna file, a thick one with numerous letters and legal papers. I kept the custody agreement on top. It was only three pages, and according to it, Trent had Jenna from a minute after midnight to midnight on holidays in alternating years. The three holidays were Christmas, Thanksgiving, and Easter.

When I came downstairs, Trent was off the phone but still shouting. This time it was between Trent and Jenna. Jenna said that he was ruining her Christmas by not letting her go watch her sister get engaged. Trent argued that it was her mother who had ruined things. The conversation ended when Jenna stormed to her room and slammed the door behind her.

Trent and I went to bed but we didn't sleep. We didn't even talk.

At five minutes after midnight, a car pulled into the driveway, crunching on the gravel until it came to a stop. Trent said, "If she wants her, she can come get her." He stayed in bed. I got up.

I didn't have to walk downstairs to Jenna's room to wake her. She had at some point relocated to the big red chair in the loft, right outside our bedroom door, across from the Christmas tree. Seeing her folded up in the chair with the comforter from her bed pulled up around her shoulders, I wanted to hug her and I wanted to cry. Instead, I touched Jenna's shoulder, woke her, and walked her down the stairs. She went out the front door with her pink travel bag bumping behind her. Doreen was waiting in the car. I closed the front door.

When I got back to bed, I didn't say anything. I lay down next to the man who wanted so little and got even less. Whenever he did get a taste, just a little one, it was snatched away. He had watched too many doors close, he had seen too many taillights shrink until they were gone.

We had talked about this when we drove back and forth between Michigan and Chicago to see each other. We had agreed that it was better to be the one leaving rather than the one left, and that it's better not to watch the taillights.

I had closed the front door quickly because I didn't want to see them. But both of us heard the fading sound of the crunch of tires on gravel as the car and Jenna drove away.

30. Almost Legal

March 2007

I don't remember how it unfolded. We would get married, but it wouldn't be legal. Trent distrusted authority; I didn't want to unite my finances with his. We would write our own vows, but say them in front of someone else to make it more real, and we would have rings to prove we had done it. The rings would be titanium. The someone else would be Elaine. The place would be her office in Chicago.

I called Elaine to schedule an appointment and tell her what we wanted to do, which she thought was a wonderful idea. We picked a date—May 5th. I went online to order the rings. I had expected that they had a stock of rings and they simply sent out what you ordered, but apparently the rings were made to order. Ours weren't too complicated so could be made on time. They would be made in Canada.

May 2007

Trent hadn't told Jenna what we were planning. Instead, he asked her if she wanted to spend the weekend with us in Chicago. She said no. We were leaving on Friday. On Thursday, a FedEx envelope arrived from the titanium-ring maker in Canada.

We took the envelope and ran upstairs, lay on the bed, and opened the envelope. Each ring was in a sheer fabric bag, closed with a slim blue ribbon that matched the color of the bag. The rings were snug but would work. Then we swapped rings so we could look at each other's. Trent's ring fit on my thumb and I twirled it around. I gave it back to him and he put both rings in his palm. He lifted my ring and placed it inside his. It fit perfectly, the smaller circle snug against the larger one.

In the city, we stayed at the Orrington, a historic hotel in Evanston. The room was large because I had reserved one big enough to include Jenna. Robin, who had led the project for which Trent had set up his construction lamp at midnight, and her husband, Keith, sent a big vase of stargazer lilies. The flowers had flung themselves open and filled the room with a heavy, heady scent.

We lay back on the bed and I turned to Trent.

"Have you written down anything that you want to say for our vows?"

"No. Have you?"

"No."

"We'll just say what is in our heart and those words will be perfect, Sweet Baby."

May 5, 2007

I drove to Elaine's, not just because I usually drove in Chicago but because Trent was sick. His stomach was roiling and he said we needed to stop at Walgreens. He was leaning back in the passenger seat, grimacing, eyes closed. I felt bad. I knew Trent was sick, literally, at the thought of making us in any way official. It had to do with good and not believing he deserved good and believing that if something good happened then something bad was sure to happen, most likely soon. I had wanted to be driven to my own wedding, even though it was about as far from the trappings of a traditional one as possible.

Trent was wearing his boots, jeans, and a light-blue "Life Is Good" T-shirt, the one that matched his eyes. I was wearing a new shirt I had bought for the occasion that was also blue, jeans, and clogs.

That morning, I had decided that I wanted flowers and cake, so I walked to Whole Foods Market and picked up white lilies and a chocolate cake with white icing. The immediate concern was Trent, who was clutching at his shirt over his abdomen because it hurt so much. We pulled into a Walgreens so he could chug half a bottle of Pepto-Bismol.

By the time we got to Elaine's, Trent had stopped grimacing. I grabbed the bags with the flowers and cake. We went inside and sat on the loveseat in the waiting room. Trent turned to me. "We're gonna get married, Sweet Baby!"

After a few minutes, Elaine popped out, squealed, "You're here!" and hugged us both.

Trent wanted to go first. He talked for a long time and I wish I could remember the exact words he used, but what I do remember is that he cried and I cried and he promised to love me forever. Then it was my turn and I made the best promise that I could.

We hugged and kissed each other and Elaine stood up and we all hugged. After we ate the cake, I asked Elaine to keep the flowers.

Back in the parking lot, we decided that we would go to Salvage One, a store I liked a lot that Trent had never seen. We walked around the three floors of rescued architectural elements, sometimes together, sometimes separately when something caught the attention of one of us. We wound up together looking at a section of flooring and Trent said he would put it in the house he would someday build for us. We hugged again and laughed that we were having our honeymoon at Salvage One.

31. Dog with a Bone

June 30, 2007

I am one of those people who can ponder things for a long time, mulling the possibilities, rolling them around, feeling one then another, like grapes rolled in a mouth.

But after that, after feeling and tasting and weighing and considering, I will decide. Most of the time, I can articulate my rationale, but not always. All I know is I have decided, and having decided, I act. If it is something I want, I want it now. I am like a dog with a bone. Or a dog that doesn't have a bone but sees one and smells one and wants one.

Sometime in July I asked Trent, "What do you think about us getting a dog?"

It was a good idea, he said, when the time was right.

The next Saturday, we were in the Jeep, headed south, driving to Ohio to look at labradoodle puppies.

The directions took us to a working farm that bred puppies for side cash. We followed the arrow on the sign at the end of the driveway that pointed us to the back. Sitting in the cool of the chilled air in the Jeep, Trent and I saw two rows of wire cages baking in the sun. Each cage held a dog. Trent and I looked at the dogs, then at each other. We didn't need to speak.

We didn't like anything about this but we had been in the car so long we might as well get out. My hair matted to my head as we walked along the cages, watching the dogs pant, noticing that not every bowl held water.

"Those are just the breeders," the owner said, and took us into the barn where some puppies rolled over each other on a blanket on a pile of straw, shaded by the high roof of the barn. She asked us which one we liked. We said we'd have to think about it.

In the Jeep on the way home, we discussed reporting the breeder. We decided against it, that no one would think the mistreatment was bad enough to require intervention. Half the dogs in Michigan were chained up in someone's front yard, Trent pointed out, and the same was probably true in Ohio.

July 7, 2007

"Hand me up one of them pups."

Trent didn't typically issue commands, certainly not to me, so I knew he had a motive. What it was was another question.

We were standing on the clean vinyl floor of a breeder's kennel. A circular temporary pen was set up in the middle of the floor, with eight squirming three-week-old labradoodle pups inside it. Trent was on one side of the pen, I was opposite him, and the breeder was between us.

I looked back at the puppy that had caught my eye—the biggest, the squirmiest. I tried to tell which one, if any, had caught Trent's eye, but couldn't. He was being intentionally noncommittal. I decided to pick up my favorite.

I reached down to the soft ball of fur, surprised at how warm it was, and handed the pup to Trent. The pup pushed his head into Trent's chest, then smelled his neck, then nibbled on his beard, which made him laugh. Trent pulled the pup back from climbing any higher up his face and passed him to me. The pup licked my cheek and I wanted to take him home right then.

After we had cycled through the rest of the pups, we met their mother, their grandfather, and few of the other dogs. After that, there didn't seem to be anything else to do so we left, telling the breeder we would think about it.

Back in the privacy of the Jeep, we first talked about how nice the place had been, how clean it was, and how healthy and happy the dogs looked. The breeder had an assistant who wore a lab coat with their logo on it. It was, at least on the surface, a world away from the breeder in Ohio.

Trent moved on to the more critical topic. "What did you think of the pups?"

"I liked them."

"Any in particular?"

"The same one you liked."

"Which one did I like?"

"The big white one. The first one. Why did you ask me to hand you one?"

"I wanted to know which one you liked."

"Was it the one you wanted to see?"

"Yep."

As soon as we got home, we called the breeder and said we were interested in the white pup with the orange collar. She said she didn't let any of them go until they were eight weeks old. That was fine, we said.

Names

I had walked out to the barn specifically to talk with Trent about a big white puppy with an orange collar. It turned out that he wanted to discuss the same thing and he launched the conversation.

"He's going to need a name."

"I've been thinking about that."

"Any names you like?"

"Moses."

"Moses?"

"Yeah, Moses. Moses was wise and he had a white beard."

"Do you think people might think it's . . ."

"Disrespectful? Well, maybe. Were there any names that you thought of?"

"Not a name, but I want it to have something to do with water."

"Water?"

"We want to take him kayaking. I want it to be a name that likes water."

"Oh. Like Nemo or something."

"That would be good."

"What would?"

"Nemo."

"Oh. I like that."

"You just said it."

"I did?"

"Yep. Nemo."

We both let the name settle in.

During his chewing stage, when Nemo would pull split logs from the woodpile and turn them into mulch, Trent called him Neminator and Shredrick, but the rest of the time he was, and still is, Nemo.

July 19, 2007

We decided that one visit was not enough of a basis to select a dog who would live with us for a decade, so three weeks later we drove back to see the pups again. They were no longer in the circular pen out front, having outgrown it, but instead in a larger kennel in the back. The assistant would bring us two of them at a time. Even though the breeder updated her website weekly with fresh photos, I was shocked at how big the puppies had gotten.

We held each of the first two, but they weren't Nemo and we weren't interested. We then asked if one of the next two could be the white one with the orange collar.

"Oh. The big one."

She came back with a black dog in one arm and a white dog twice his size in the other. Nemo. Trent held him and told him his name. I held him and buried my nose in his soft fur.

The assistant offered to bring out the next pair. We told her not to bother.

After the required number of weeks, on August 11th we went back to the breeder, picked up Nemo, and took him home. When we got there, we set him on the grass. The first thing he did was piddle. The second thing he did was curl up on his back, tuck his paws across his belly, and fall asleep.

August 12, 2007

The Newaygo night is black as tar when the moon goes missing. If I had turned toward Trent—we were in bed and Nemo was in his crate downstairs—I wouldn't have been able to see him, so I didn't bother.

We were both flat on our backs. My eyes were open, I didn't know about Trent's. My words came out without thinking.

"Jenna's going to move in with us."

"Why do you say that?"

"Because of Nemo. Now she knows she can count on us staying together. We're a family."

"We were a family before. We have a house."

"A house is just a house. A dog is a family."

Trent didn't say anything more and I knew why—he didn't want to get his hopes up.

32. Negotiations

November 2007

Things hadn't been going well between Jenna and her mom. In a moment of anger and exasperation, Doreen threatened to send Jenna to live with her father. Whether rising to the challenge or calling her bluff, Jenna responded, "Fine!"

Trent and Doreen had several conversations and Jenna acted out a few more times. Negotiations were testy on both sides. The challenge Trent had was the same one we had for the Newaygo house—the inability to walk away.

Trent missed his daughter, he wanted her with him, and he could not let Doreen know this. She would willingly suffer through Jenna's acting out for the pleasure of withholding from Trent what he wanted most.

I watched Trent on the phone with Doreen, talking tough, making demands, saying that he wasn't sure he wanted Jenna, given the way she had been acting. Every call ended with him angrily flipping his phone shut. Then he would stand there, head down, chewing a fingernail, hoping he had played his cards correctly. He chewed his thumbs until they bled.

The agreement was forged with guidance from legal counsel on both sides. Jenna was coming to live with us. She would arrive in time for the start of the second term at school. Trent insisted that she arrive on Saturday. He was still laying down his cards. He knew the game was still on.

On Friday night, Doreen called. Jenna had done something that made her mother very angry and would certainly have made Trent angry if it had happened in our house.

We were quiet as we lay in bed that night. I knew what was going through Trent's mind. He was treasuring the hope that his daughter would live with him and preparing himself for the possibility that his carefully played cards might be swept off the table at the last moment. He was afraid she was going to be brought close only to be taken from him once again. He was also worried about her.

I stayed quiet until he spoke.

"I don't know, Sweet Baby."

"Don't know what?"

"Don't know what kind of shape Jenna's going to be in when she gets here."

"I'm not worried."

"You're not?" He said it accusingly, as if I were missing an important parental gene. But I wasn't worried and I told him why.

"Jenna is just making sure her mother doesn't change her mind at the last minute. She wants to live with us."

He didn't say anything. He was hoping I was right. Rolling over on my side, away from him, I hoped he wasn't going to ask me to substantiate my statement. I couldn't.

We lay in bed, both awake but not speaking. My back was to him, the soles of my feet on his fuzzy right calf. His arms were behind his head. We were both wondering and hoping—was Jenna coming to live with us tomorrow?

December 1, 2007

Saturday was one of those days where you do small things to fill the time while you wait for the big thing but your mind is not on the small things you are doing. Your mind is on what you're waiting for. We were waiting for Jenna.

I don't know what Trent was thinking about because we weren't talking. We didn't want to do or say anything that might disturb all those carefully played cards.

I was thinking about all those nights I had held him in bed, when he would lie on his back and the tears would run from his eyes to his ears and he would ask, "Why can't I have you both?" I would always answer the same way.

"You can, Sweet Baby. Just not right now."

Jenna and her mom were supposed to arrive by noon and that was pretty much when they got there. That had been one of Trent's cards—he needed to have a set time because he wasn't sure he would be home. Based on what I had been hearing about what had been going on at Doreen's house, I expected a loud, angry, and quick separation. That wasn't what happened.

We heard them pull into the driveway and we went out onto the porch, ready to catch, embrace, or wrangle Jenna, depending on what the situation required. Jenna and Doreen got out of the car and hugged each other for a really long time. After several minutes Trent said, "I'm not going to stand here and watch them make out." We went back inside.

We sat at the small teak dining room table and waited. We still didn't speak. Then, suddenly, Jenna came through the front door, long brown hair flying behind her, pink gym bag hanging from her bent elbow, bulging white plastic grocery bags in both hands. Somehow, even with her load, Jenna managed to slam the front door. She marched past us into her room and slammed that door, too. Hard. A piece of molding fell off the door.

Trent hollered, "You break it, you fix it."

Then Trent and I stood up and hugged each other, Trent swallowing me up in his arms. I could feel his joy wrapped all around me and I thought of something he had written once, on one of the notes left in the Chicago kitchen: "My heart is so happy we could both dance around inside it." It felt as though, if there were just a touch more pressure from his arms, I would pass through his skin and into his heart and we would both dance. When we looked at each other again, Trent's eyes were wet. Then he pulled me into his chest again.

"I have you both. I have you both. I have you both."

The next morning, Trent showed Jenna how to repair the molding. Jenna hammered the nails carefully and cleanly, and Trent was proud of her.

December 3, 2007

Trent took Jenna to school on her first day. She was a transfer student, starting on the first day of the winter quarter. They were both a little nervous.

As Trent walked Jenna into the building, two girls came running up to her. "You must be Jenna!" They had met on the school's Facebook page and let her know that Friday was Silly Hat Day. On Friday Jenna wore her silly hat—a long stocking cap—and looked adorable.

I had been uncertain how to refer to Jenna.

"Jenna, what should I call you? Neither of us likes step-daughter."

"Call me your EP."

"EP?"

"Yeah. EP. Extra Package. That's what my friend and her stepmom call each other."

"Hmm. I like the extra part. That sounds like a bonus, an extra benefit. But I'm not sure I like the package part."

Jenna just looked at me, waiting.

"It could be nice but it could also be a burden—like a heavy package."

Jenna continued to say nothing.

"What about present? Extra Present. That sounds like a good thing. What do you think?"

"Yeah, that's okay."

I knew that was all she was going to say. My goal then became to talk until I made her eyes roll.

"Okay, so EP. is Extra Present. Or it could be . . . Extraordinary Person. That's not bad, either."

Still no reaction.

"Or maybe Exquisite Princess. That's good, too."

Jenna's eyes rolled and she buried her face in the couch pillow.

Score!

Later in the term, Trent and I went to the parent-teacher conference. We had been tracking Jenna's grades on the school's website and Jenna was doing well, with one exception. After meeting all her teachers, we understood why.

As Trent said when we left the teacher's classroom, "What a dick."

The great thing about a small school is you can do any extracurricular activity you want because the school doesn't have enough students to field a team or fill the slots of another activity. Want to be a cheerleader? Fine. What to be in the band? Fine. Want to run track? Fine.

Jenna debated between track and softball. Even though she was better at track, she chose softball because she would be part of a team. She batted .000, but if she was walked to first base she could steal her way home. She was fast.

April–May 2008

Trent noticed it first but didn't say anything until I noticed it. He waited until he found me bent over the aquarium, focused on Ginger's shell.

"Do you see it?"

"I do. Is that a hole?"

"Looks like it."

"How long has it been there?"

"Maybe a couple weeks."

"Has it gotten bigger?"

"Seems like it."

Neither of us thought a hole in Ginger's shell was a good thing, but neither of us was inclined to take her to a vet. One morning a few weeks later, we found Ernest on his big rock under the heat lamp, stretched out on top of Ginger. It didn't seem that he was trying to crush her. It seemed, at least to us, that he was trying to comfort her. When Trent lifted him off, though, Ginger didn't move. Trent touched her legs. They didn't move.

He didn't want to bury her. He said she came from water and should go back to water. So he cut a thin, broad piece of pine that would serve as a funeral raft and we went down to the river. After saying a few words, he laid Ginger on her raft and put it on the surface of the Muskegon. The current swept the raft downstream, and after just a few minutes, a little wave at the edge of the bank licked Ginger off the raft.

"Did you see that, Sweet Baby! The river took her!"

I thought back to a news report we had seen on television a few weeks earlier, where a badly wounded bird had been found and nursed back to life. Trent had looked displeased.

"Shouldn't they have saved the bird?" I asked him.

"Just took a good meal from a healthy animal that needs to eat."

I looked at him, surprised at his seeming heartlessness.

"Everything you eat had to die for you to eat it. Death is a part of life, Sweet Baby."

June 2008

A boy asked Jenna to the prom and Trent went on the alert.

"With who?"

"Warbly.*"

"What kind of name is Warbly?"

"It's his name, Dad. Anyway, I'm going."

"What year is he?"

"Senior."

"You're not going."

"Why not?"

"Because he's a senior and you're a sophomore."

"Mom says it's fine."

"It's not fine and I say you can't go and you're living with me."

"I am too going."

"You're not going."

"Why not?"

"You know why not."

"You're just saying that because you were like that."

"Yes I was. All boys are like that."

"He's not."

"You don't know him."

"He loves me."

"Loves you? You for sure are not going. He doesn't love you."

"You don't know him."

"I know him."

"I know what you're thinking. Say it."

"I don't need to say it."

"You think he wants to have sex with me."

"I know he wants to have sex with you."

"He does not and I'm going. Mom says it's fine."

"Fine. If she thinks it's fine, I will drive you to your mother's house and he can pick you up from there. He is not getting you from this house."

"No, Dad, You can't do that!"

"The hell I can't. He loves you? If he loves you, he'll come get you."

"He will come get me. He loves me!"

"He doesn't love you and he's not going to come get you. He going to take someone else and he's going to have sex with her."

"You're wrong!"

Jenna fled to her bedroom and slammed the door. She had done a good job previously of nailing on the molding and it didn't fall off. But Trent was right. Warbly didn't drive to Battle Creek and he did take someone else to the prom.

33. Empty Nest

June 7, 2008

At the end of the school year, Jenna demanded to move back in with her mother. I didn't understand. She seemed happy. She'd had a sleepover with lots of friends for whom Trent had made pancakes at one in the morning. We had painted the walls of her bedroom the bright yellow that she wanted and she had covered them with photos and posters. She appeared settled in and satisfied.

Trent said she wanted to go back to Battle Creek so that there wouldn't be an adult watching over her. When school let out for the summer, he drove her back to her mother's. In July, he and Jenna met once for lunch, to talk about where she would live in the fall, where she would go to school.

"How are you going to make it worth my while to move back in with you?" she asked him.

"We'll love you, we'll feed you, you'll have a place to sleep, but you'll still have to do the dishes."

Doing the dishes was something we all did together. Jenna declined the offer.

When Trent got home he was both angry and sad. He said that he couldn't let his daughter call the shots but saying what he'd said and not giving in was the hardest thing he'd ever done.

June 29, 2008

We needed to let Ernest go, Trent said. Ernest was big enough to survive in the wild, but if we kept him any longer he would lose the ability to fend for himself.

I thought about all the time we'd spent with Ernest, from when he was so tiny in the white enamel roaster, to the fish tank in Chicago, to the bigger fish tank in Newaygo. We kept the tank right next to the dining room table and I liked watching him swim.

Trent got a five-gallon white bucket, put some water from the aquarium in it, and added Ernest. I got on the back of the three-wheeler and held the bucket as Trent slipped onto the driver's saddle.

We stood at the edge of the swamp and said our good-byes. I wondered how Ernest would feel about swimming through water that had seeds and leaves and who knew what else. Trent put his hand down to the water and Ernest jumped in without hesitating. He went under immediately. We never saw him resurface, though we waited awhile.

July 26, 2008

Since that first expedition on Tamarack Creek, Trent and I had become good kayakers. We practiced on the Muskegon, then ventured out onto smaller, faster rivers. We kayaked before the leaves came out on the trees and after they were long gone. If the river wasn't completely frozen, we were on it.

For his birthday that summer, we went to the Sturgeon River, near Wolverine in Michigan. We went up on a Thursday and stayed at Malone's because Trent loved the four hand-built cabins. He kayaked every day and I did every other day. I had given him a waterproof camera, and on the days he soloed, he brought back countless pictures of what he had seen, some from above water and some from below.

We knew we were good kayakers. The section of the Sturgeon River we traveled dumps three of every four kayakers, but it didn't dump me and it dumped Trent only once, when he was helping someone caught in the rocks.

Trent preferred pie to cake, and in the tiny cabin kitchen on his birthday, I made his favorite—raspberry—with berries he had gotten from his favorite berry growers near the house at Mud Lake. In the top crust, I used the tip of a knife to make a drawing of him kayaking. He cut two slices carefully, preserving his favorite part of the drawing.

We drove back to Newaygo late on Sunday afternoon because I needed to be in Chicago for work on Monday. When I returned to Newaygo on Wednesday night, the pie was still in the refrigerator, with the same two pieces missing. When I asked Trent why he hadn't eaten any more of the pie, he said he hadn't felt like it.

August 5, 2008

Trent was in Newaygo and I was again in Chicago for client work. It was night. One of us called the other, I don't remember which. From the way he sounded, though, I knew he was in a bad place.

It wasn't that he sounded angry or sad. He was instead despondent. Hopeless. Helpless. He mentioned in an offhand way that it might be good time to die. Jenna had gone back to live with her mother, I was in Chicago, he was alone. He was technically sitting in the garage as we spoke, but he had clearly fallen into the black hole. Deep.

I tried to get him to think about something in the future that he could look forward to but to no avail. Anything I proposed was dismissed. My coming home was two days and too far away. I decided to focus on the present and suggested that he think of all the people and things he loved, write each one on a piece of paper, and put them in a glass jar. Trent had some nice antique minnow jars made out of glass that was old and watery. They were large and fragile and had an indentation near the rim to secure the wire bands that attached to the lines that kept the jars from floating away when they were put in the water. Whenever I carried one, I used both hands. I encouraged him to find one and start filling it. He liked the idea.

When I got home later that week, he was still there. He had made it.

August 16, 2008

I woke up and looked over at Trent. He looked troubled, his arms behind his head, his eyes staring at the ceiling. I hadn't asked in a long time but it seemed relevant, so I asked as gently as I could.

"Sweet Baby, do you want to kill yourself this morning?"

Trent's eyes looked away toward the window behind his shoulder. He brought them back to me before answering.

"No."

He was lying.

"Okay," was all I said as I rolled back onto my pillow. I stared at the ceiling and wondered what was going to happen to us. He had said, "As long as we keep loving each other and telling each other the truth, we're going to be all right." He had also just lied. Did this mean that we were no longer going to be all right?

August 18, 2008

It was morning and I was sitting in bed, frustrated because I wanted to be able to look out the window and see the sky, at least a bit of it, but instead all I could see was pine trees. I went outside, determined to identify which trees were blocking my view of the sky.

Later that day, I explained to Trent what I wanted, and showed him the four trees that I thought needed to come down. He looked from the trees to our bedroom window and said it might take more than four. That week, I was in Chicago again, and Trent and I spoke every night. One night he said he and the two neighbor boys who worked with him once in a while, Justin and Jeremy, had taken down the trees—eleven of them.

When I got home, Trent took me upstairs. When I looked out the window, I saw stars.

COMING APART

34. Shifting

August 2008

The way we were living wasn't sustainable, given how often I was in Chicago for client work, so I started searching for alternative income sources. I joined Triiibes.com, an online community, to figure out how to make money in the woods of Newaygo. I signed up for an online marketing program.

In it, we were assigned to small groups, theoretically six of us. For our first virtual meeting, though, only one person showed up. Her business was giving tarot card readings. I wasn't sure how I felt about the tarot, and whether I could help someone with their business when I didn't know if I believed in it. So I asked her to give me a reading.

"There's been a betrayal," were the first words out of her mouth, which shocked me, because earlier that day one of my colleagues had said to me, "I feel as if I've been betrayed." I hadn't heard the word *betrayal* in years and now I had heard it twice in one day. I shifted my attitude toward her business from dismissive to neutral but added a generous measure of salt.

Newspaper

Trent sat at the dining room table in Newaygo with an opened newspaper. He read aloud—an obituary of a man in his forties who had died of a heart attack. He then told me about a friend who had had one at forty-two but who had lived. The preoccupation made me uncomfortable but I didn't say anything. I hoped it would pass.

Time Together

I had been working long hours for some time. One evening, after a long workday, I decided to spend a little time in Triiibes to decompress and perhaps find a way to escape the long hours. When I came upstairs, I told Trent a joke I'd read that I'd found rather funny. He didn't laugh.

"Where did you hear that?"

"On Triiibes."

"This is what you were doing when we could have been spending time together?"

Another River

Toward the end of August, we headed up toward White Cloud, to a river that Trent had been on before but I hadn't. Trent explained to the outfitter that we didn't need equipment—we had our own—but did need transportation back to our vehicle from the exit point. The outfitter described the options. A variety of entrance and exit points allowed for different trip lengths—two, three, six, or nine hours.

I checked my watch. It was just after eight in the morning, so I expected Trent to choose the six-hour trip. It was a nice day and the river was wide and easy. The outfitter needed to know where to drop us and where to pick us up.

"So which one do you want to do? How many hours?"

Normally Trent would check with me before responding, to make sure we were on the same page. This time he didn't.

"Three."

I looked at him, one eyebrow raised.

"We'll take it slow," he said.

This was the first time I thought that something was wrong with Trent and that he knew it.

We did take it slow. We stopped to look at flowers and Trent took innumerable pictures of a hornets' nest, with the camera I'd given him for his birthday. I picked up little stones and Trent asked to see them. Holding them in the broad palm of one hand and rubbing the fingers of his other hand across the stones, he said, "Sweet Baby, you always find the best rocks."

Him Again

It was late and I was tired. I was sitting up in bed, waiting for Trent to finish brushing his teeth. But instead of getting in bed, he started pacing at the foot of the bed. I watched him, trying to decide what to say when he spoke.

"You're going to go back to him."

"What?"

"You heard me. You're just going to go back to him."

"To who?"

"Your old husband. When I'm not here you're just going to go back to him."

I fell back on the bed and sighed. "You still don't know me at all."

The argument was in his head and I could say or do nothing to fight it. Trent slowly came to bed. I put my hand on his chest and curled up against him.

Tarot Reading

In early September, I decided to ask the woman in the marketing class for another tarot reading. I was looking to any source for answers, for a way out of my being gone so much and Trent's being so unhappy. The only sound was the soft click of each card hitting the table and then a pause. She said, more to herself than to me, "No, this can't be right," and I heard the cards being shuffled again, then the click, click again of cards being placed on the table.

She started talking to herself again, then to me. "This can't be . . . no, this isn't you, this is Trent. This is about Trent. Trent is sick. Trent is sick and . . . and he knows it. Something is very wrong with him. You need to get him to a doctor. He won't want to go but knows something is wrong."

That night, I looked at Trent a little more closely than I usually did. He was laughing as he made dinner, he moved the heavy cast iron skillet as if it were a paper plate. The tarot woman had gotten this one wrong. I didn't take what she said with a grain of salt; I blew it right off the table. If she had ever met Trent, ever seen him, she would know that he was big and strong and had a laugh that could shake the walls of the garage. He had also just had a physical two months earlier. Other than his hypertension, which was being well maintained with meds, he was fine. She was quite simply wrong.

Taking Nemo

When I woke up, Trent was already awake, standing at the bedroom window in his boxer briefs, looking out toward the barn. He didn't turn to me as he spoke.

"When I'm gone and we don't live here anymore, you can't take Nemo with you. He can't live his life on a leash."

"What are you talking about?"

"Promise me that when I'm gone and you move back to Chicago, you won't take Nemo with you."

"I'm not going to promise you. That dog is going to be long dead before we don't live here anymore."

"Promise me."

"This is stupid."

"Promise me!"

So I did, in a very snotty voice because I thought he was being ridiculous.

"I promise you that when you're gone and we don't live here anymore that I won't take Nemo with me because he can't live his life on a leash."

"Good."

I fell back on the pillows, worried despite myself. Trent was overly preoccupied with his own death again but it felt different than when he talked about suicide. I thought about asking him about it, why he was talking this way, whether he was worried, but I was afraid so I didn't.

September Weekend

I was in Chicago for work and would be there for a week and a half. Trent had followed, taking the Amtrak from Grand Rapids to Chicago, so we could spend the weekend in the city. We had never done this before.

The trains were delayed six hours, but once he finally got there, we had a great time. One night we saw *Wicked,* billed as the untold story of the witches of Oz, and sat in the first row of the balcony. At the climactic end of Act 1, I looked over at Trent. He was sitting forward in his seat, watching and listening, not just with his eyes and ears but with his entire being. At the end of the show he said, about the wicked witch of the West, "She was green because of her father." I didn't understand. He explained, "Her father made her mother drink the green liquid and that's what made her green."

After the show, we visited with Steven and his wife and spent the night there. Lying on their sofa bed, Trent and I made love very slowly and very quietly, one of those times when we looked in each other's eyes and never looked away.

Late Sunday afternoon, I dropped Trent off at Union Station so he could catch the train back to Michigan. I watched his blond head and Carhartt sweatshirt–covered shoulders disappear into the crowd, which was like a river flowing toward the station doors.

He called me Sunday night, not from Newaygo but from a friend's house in the far western suburbs of Chicago. The Amtrak hadn't been running because of a flood in Indiana. Trent knew I had a big day on Monday so visited the friend rather than coming back to the hotel room. The trains weren't running on Monday, either, so Trent ended up taking the bus, an eight-hour ordeal.

On Tuesday, the electrician came to install a ceiling light in the entry foyer. Trent told me about this, told me I was going to like it, and added that the excavator would be coming Wednesday. Trent wanted to make some changes to the driveway by the front of the house. The excavator would sculpt the area where Trent and I would plant hydrangeas (on the shady side, for me) and grasses (on the sunny side, for Trent).

35. Blue

Wednesday, September 17, 2008

I called Trent when I left Chicago. Usually I leave around five thirty, or four thirty if I'm lucky. This time I was leaving early, around two thirty. I had met with a client who was normally out in the suburbs but this time was in the city for a training program she was shepherding. We met downtown in the morning. I stayed for lunch, then left.

Traffic looked bad so I called Trent to tell him I wasn't sure exactly how long it would take me to get home. At I-94 exit 27, I picked up a sandwich from Panera and paid for it with a gift card plus two pennies. Just outside of Grand Rapids, I called Trent again to let him know I was forty-five minutes away. It was a few minutes before six o'clock.

I told him about the gift card and the two cents and he laughed—he loved a good deal. He told me about the excavation and said that when I saw it I was going to think it was beautiful. I was a half hour from home.

When I pulled into the driveway, I heard the familiar crunch of the gravel. As I came through the trees I could see the excavation work. He was right, it was beautiful.

As the car moved forward, I was looking back to where we were going to plant the hydrangeas and the grasses when I caught something in my left peripheral vision. It was Justin, one of the teenage neighbors who helped us out from time to time. He was running, his blond hair flapping, his eyes big. I hit the switch to lower the window as he came up to the Jeep.

"Trent's down! He's down. He's blue!"

I threw open the door and ran. Trent's legs were on the concrete pad in front of the garage, his torso and head were on the gravel. He was face up, facing the garage, the house was off to his right. His right knee was up, his left leg straight, and his foot turned outward. He was wearing his boots, thick socks, jean shorts, and a white T-shirt with colorful but faded graphics that he got from volunteering at a Battle Creek event. His wire-rimmed glasses were on the gravel, by his right hand. The T-shirt (they had given him two, because he was so helpful) was one of his favorites.

Justin was right. Trent was blue, as if someone had painted his face with blue watercolor, from the inside. Because his head was blue but the rest of him normal, it looked as if someone had snapped his head off at the neck and snapped on a blue replacement. This made me think he had broken his neck. If he had been up on the roof, I was going to be really mad at him. Justin interrupted my thoughts (and probably snapped me back into reality).

"I called 9-1-1."

I kneeled on the gravel and leaned over Trent's face to feel his breath on my cheek. I felt nothing. I put my finger on his neck to feel for a pulse but couldn't find one. I poked at his arm to see whether it was soft or stiff. It was soft and warm so I did what I remembered of CPR, from when I was a hospital dental hygienist.

Five compressions followed by one breath. I did it that way a few times before I remembered that the ratio is different for a single rescuer. So I switched to fifteen compressions and two breaths. I think Justin was moving behind me because I kept hearing the crunch of gravel.

On one of the compressions, as I pressed the heel of my clasped hands into Trent's chest, I heard a little crack and knew I had just broken off his xiphoid process, the little spur of bone that sticks down from the bottom of the sternum. That meant with every subsequent compression I would be lacerating his diaphragm.

Trent's mouth and lips were flaccid. It was much easier to get a good seal than on the hard plastic lips of the Resusci Anne we had in CPR class. When I blew in, I could feel my breath go into his lungs, I could see his chest rise. On the exhalation, I could smell the beer he had been drinking. I took deep breaths before I blew—he must have had big lungs because they needed a lot of air.

A man came with a little yellow plastic box and took over the compressions. I stayed with the breathing. Justin said again, "I called 9-1-1." The man—I had no idea who he was—said they would be here soon. He and I maintained the 15:2 ratio, and I figured the CPR rules must have changed.

On one exhale, a little of what was either drool or spit-up came out of Trent's mouth and I thought he was coming back to life, but it was only spit-up. Another time, on the rest between breaths, when the man was pressing on Trent's chest, I screamed. On another rest, I talked into Trent's ear, "You can come back or you can go, but if you're coming back, you're coming back all the way. I can't live with you in a bed all the time." Something about me saying this seemed to affect the man doing the compressions but I couldn't tell what he thought.

I heard the siren of an ambulance getting louder. Good. The man with the yellow box kept pressing and I kept blowing. I was glad he was there. CPR is much easier with two people. On one of the breaths, with my head down, I could hear the siren growing fainter and I thought, *They're turning away. They're lost!* I kept blowing into Trent's lungs. I didn't know what to do to make the ambulance come back.

Then the sirens got louder again. The man and I kept working. Just when they got as loud as they had been before, they started growing fainter again. They were lost.

I wanted to tell Justin to go down to the end of the driveway, to signal the ambulance, but all I could do was count the presses the man made and be ready to breathe into Trent again.

36. Leaving

I looked into Trent's eyes to see whether I could tell whether he was still there. I couldn't see anything in his eyes, but I had a feeling he could hear me. On a rest between breaths, I said, "You don't need to stay. Jenna and I will be okay. And you'll be able to watch over both of us. You can have us both."

Then the ambulance was there. The man and I kept doing our pressing and breathing. People got out and started laying things on the ground around Trent. Then they told us they would take over, and they did. I looked at the man who had been doing the compressions for the first time. He was young, maybe twenty-five or so, and he looked scared.

Nemo had been sitting quietly by Trent's head the whole time. The man had been to Trent's right, by his chest, doing the compressions. I had been to Trent's left, by his head, doing the breaths. Nemo was on the other side of Trent's head, watching. Nemo never moved. He never barked. He had been sitting there when I ran up from the Jeep, but I wasn't really paying attention to him.

When the ambulance people started laying bags and equipment by Trent's body, Nemo grabbed one of the bags and started to run away with it. One of the EMTs yelled, "Get that dog out of here!"

I got Nemo and I don't know how I did that—I have never been able to catch him at full stride, so he must have slowed or stopped. I grabbed his collar and took him into the house. Justin's mother told me later that Nemo stayed at the front window the whole time, watching.

The emergency people were all around Trent when I got back from putting Nemo in the house, but there was room by Trent's left arm so I went there.

"Ma'am, I'm going to have to ask you to step away."

"I'm not leaving him."

"You're interfering with his care."

I was not. I wasn't in anybody's way.

"Have you ever given CPR to your husband?" I said angrily.

"No, but I've given it to my daughter."

"I'm not leaving."

She walked away and then moved to Trent's other side.

"Was alcohol a factor?" she asked, of no one in particular.

I looked at her blankly. She sniffed the air as if she were Sherlock Holmes.

"Yes! Alcohol was a factor!" she announced.

I ignored her. I got up, I think to talk on the phone, I think to Justin's mother. When I went back, the space where I had been was filled. I looked down and could see that Trent wasn't there anymore. The words just came out.

"He's gone."

One of the emergency men looked up at me and said, "No, ma'am, there's still hope."

I leaned over, looked into Trent's face, and said, "Hear that, Sweet Baby? There's still hope."

But I felt stupid after I said it because I knew he was already gone. I had told him it was okay for him to go, but I wasn't ready for him to leave.

Shock

As they continued to work on Trent, I suddenly remembered the warning from the tarot card reader. She was right—this is what she had been talking about. In an odd way, though, the knowledge gave me a little peace.

The emergency technicians had a little yellow and black box—was it the same yellow box the man had brought? It was connected to Trent and it told the emergency people—literally, aloud—what to do.

"Shock indicated."

The EMTs applied shock.

"Testing vital signs."

The box waited a bit.

"Shock indicated."

They shocked him again.

"Testing vital signs."

I waited.

"Shock not indicated."

I have fainted from time to time in my life—always when I am donating blood, so I know the warning signs.

"I'm going down," I mumbled.

This prompted the woman I'd disagreed with earlier to get behind me and hold me up. Apparently she and I had more to disagree about.

"Let me down."

"I'm trying to keep you from hitting your head."

"I'm not going to hit my head. But if you don't let me go down I'll faint and then I'll hit my head."

She slowly released me and I slid down her shins to sit on the gravel, then leaned back to rest my head. It felt good to be lying down. I could hear the little box talking, testing vital signs.

"Shock not indicated."

Some of the people were now around me instead of Trent but I don't know who they were. One may have been Justin.

A different emergency woman came over to me. She wasn't wearing a yellow jacket like the others. She had brown hair and wore a white shirt and black pants that made me assume she was in charge. She started to say something and then stopped.

"I'll wait until you're feeling better."

"Tell me now."

She hesitated.

"If you wait until I'm better and standing up I might go down again. I'm in the perfect position. Tell me now."

The woman I didn't like was standing off to my left side. Trent was lying to my right. I looked up at the woman in the white shirt. A section of her hair was blowing in the light wind and she tucked it behind her ear.

"He has expired. I'm sorry."

Saying Good-Bye

I stood up and walked the few steps over to Trent. His knee was down—one of the EMT workers must have straightened his leg, or else it just went to the ground with all the CPR compressions. His T-shirt had come up and his belly was sticking up—his stomach bloated with air from the CPR. I pulled his shirt down but it wouldn't cover his belly and I felt bad for him, lying there so exposed.

The EMTs told me the medical examiner would be there in forty-five minutes, that because it was an unwitnessed death, he had to come.

One of my best friends had died in an accident when we were in our twenties, so I knew how little time we had left together. I knew how I wanted to spend it.

I moved to his side and lay down next to him, putting my left hand in his cupped right hand and my right on his chest, just as I would have if we were upstairs in our bed. His chest still felt strong and the blond and gray hairs of his chest still curled around my fingers. I smelled his neck, which smelled like his shaving cream. He must have shaved for me. I looked at the little hairs that grew out of the mole by his ear, the short spikes that he kept so neatly trimmed. I rubbed the tip of my nose on his T-shirt.

The emergency people had a few questions for me so I stood up, reluctantly. They asked about Trent's family. I wanted to go see Jenna, to tell her, I said.

"You can't."

"No?"

"It's two hours away and you just fainted. You're not capable of driving that far."

They were right. I thought about calling her but decided to wait.

I went to lie down again next to Trent. His face was less blue and I thought, *He's coming back!* Then I realized what it was. *No, he's not. That's just the blood draining out of his face to the back of his head.* I noticed his tongue sticking out between his teeth on the side. I tried to push it back, but couldn't, so I looked away. I put my left hand back in his right, feeling his calluses again, and my right hand back on his chest. I lay there for a long time. It was starting to get dark and the air was cooler.

The skin of Trent's chest seemed to grow warm under my hand and I wondered whether it might be him, trying to physically connect with me one last time, or simply my own body heat radiating back to me.

Justin spoke. "The medical examiner is here." I stood up.

We stepped into the garage and the medical examiner asked a lot of questions about Trent's health and his family. I answered them all honestly. The examiner told me that because Trent and I weren't married, I would have no say in what happened to his body. He explained that Trent's daughter would have no say, either, because she was not yet eighteen. The only people who would were his parents. He was, he said, only asking the question to know my preference. He asked me whether I wanted an autopsy. I did. I wanted to know what had happened.

37. Slow Motion

The medical examiner left the garage to do his work with Trent. I used the cell phone lying on the workbench and called Jenna. When she answered, I asked if I could speak to her mother and told Jenna to put on some comfortable clothes. When Doreen got on the phone, I told her that I had something important to tell Jenna, but didn't know whether it was better if I told her over the phone, or if I told Doreen and Doreen told Jenna in person.

"Tell me, and I'll decide."

"Trent is dead."

"What?"

"Trent is dead."

"How?"

"I don't know. When I came home he was lying in the driveway. His face was blue."

She said nothing.

I filled the space. "It might have been a heart attack."

Doreen paused to consider, then decided. "You can tell her."

"Okay."

I didn't know whether this was a good idea and I knew I was in no condition to have an opinion. I waited for Jenna.

"Yeah?"

"I have something . . . difficult to tell you."

Her response was soft, wary. "Yeah?"

"Jenna, your dad died."

"He did?"

"Yes."

"How?"

"I don't know."

It came back as a wail. "You don't know?"

"No. When I came home he was lying in the driveway and his face was blue."

"But you don't know?"

"We won't know for sure what happened unless they do an autopsy, and it's up to your grandparents whether that happens."

"It hurts so bad, it hurts so bad, it hurts so bad, it hurts so bad!"

I didn't know what to say. I wanted to hold her but she wasn't there.

"It does. I'm sorry."

"Where is he?"

"He's gone. They took his body away."

The wail came back into her voice. "Where is it?"

"I don't know. They took it away in the ambulance."

"I have to go now."

She hung up.

Justin and Kim, Justin's mother, were the only people left. I hugged Justin good-bye and told him I was glad that he had called 9-1-1, that I wasn't sure I would have been able to do it. I hugged Kim and turned down her offer to stay at their house for the night. I would be all right on my own, I told them. I just needed to lie down.

I got my things from Chicago out of the car. I didn't want to bother but also didn't want to leave my laptop out there. I made my way carefully up to the front stairs of the house. When you live in the country and there are no lights, what they say is true—if you hold your arm straight out in front of you, you can't see your hand. I turned the doorknob and went inside, flipping on the newly installed foyer light switch. The glare was much too bright and I made a mental note to find a less intense bulb in the morning.

Dropping my bags, I went into the kitchen, grabbed onto the counter of the sink, and wailed. It was a strange, plaintive, moaning, howling sound, like what Trent and I had heard one night in bed when coyotes had banded together and killed a deer.

Donation

A woman from the organ and tissue donation program called and asked whether it was an okay time to answer a few questions about Trent. I was sitting at the dining room table and turned my hand over to look at my watch. Eleven twenty. I told her it was fine. Apparently it's a good time for a lot of people.

She asked me whether Trent had ever traveled abroad. She asked about his medications. She asked something—I don't remember what—that reminded me that Trent had always wanted to see the Amazon rainforest but never had, and I started to cry.

The woman didn't say anything. She just waited. I made a mental note to be silent when grieving people are crying.

After the call, I decided to go to bed, but not in our bed upstairs. I would sleep in Jenna's bed, the bed I'd bought after my divorce, the bed that made me feel safe. As I started to get in under the covers, I screamed again, but not from emotional pain.

My knees were dark red, dented, and swollen. It took me awhile to figure out why. It was the CPR. I wondered vaguely which was worse—kneeling on gravel or on concrete. In the middle of the night I woke up, dizzy. I held on to the sides of the bed so I wouldn't fall out.

September 18, 2008

In the morning I woke with relief, glad to be at last out of a terrible nightmare, that Trent was dead. Then, with a horror that came at me from the front and pulled me out the back, like the ocean riptide I'd gotten caught in once, I remembered that it wasn't a dream and I howled again. I was the deer being killed by coyotes and my cry ended the same way, muffled and whimpering.

Sometime later I went into the kitchen. On the counter was a white bag of apples. Trent must have gone to the grocery store on his last day. I opened the fridge and found his other purchases, grapefruit juice, milk, a roast, and five pounds of bacon. He was going to cook us a roast. He was going to make bacon and eggs.

I walked upstairs to look at our bed. It was made but the pillows weren't neatly in place. Trent hadn't made the bed. The woman who sometimes cleaned our house had been there. Neither Trent nor I like to clean. He was making sure the house was ready for me when I came home. I walked outside and noticed that the grass was freshly cut. That would have been Justin's work.

I didn't want to go into the garage. His captain's chair was pulled up to his workbench. The can of beer was half full. A photograph lay on the workbench. Trent must have been looking at it. It was the one of Trent and Jenna and me. The only one. It made me cry so I turned to the stack of papers instead.

I picked up an envelope addressed to Trent from Baker College, which had caught my eye a week earlier. He had started attending Baker when he wanted to learn how to use a computer but had ended up a pre-college student, with two classes each semester. When I had asked him about the envelope, he had said something like, "It's not yours." His words felt harsh but I agreed with him; it was mail for him, not me.

The envelope contained a letter that said the college had received his request to reinstate his academic eligibility. It included a copy of his explanation for his failed term after having been on the Dean's List the term before. I liked the way he wrote it, plainly. He said that his daughter had moved out and that had been hard for him. I cried some more.

Looking up from the paper, I noticed a baby food jar I had never seen before with strips of paper in it. When I saw that the paper had Trent's writing on it, I cried again. He hadn't used one of his big minnow jars, he had used a baby food jar. The jar was never going to be easy to deal with. I unscrewed the cap and laid the thin strips of paper out on the workbench.

Otis

F Drive South

Mud Lk Road

O.T. Johnson

the good years at Ralston's

my vision

time with Jenna

Gary Rapp

Toyota Land Cruncher

It was a list not just of what Trent had loved, but of what he had loved and lost. His dog, the house on F Drive where he had thrown a massive Super Bowl party in the great red barn, his beloved swamp, and people he loved, including his best friend, Steven's brother, who had killed himself with alcohol and a car.

I picked up the can of beer, went back into the house, and put the can in the freezer because I couldn't throw it away and I couldn't leave it there and it was evidence that Trent had been there and that he had been alive.

About half past six, I went outside again, wanting to see what Trent saw before he died. The bit of blood on the gravel must have come from a needle put into Trent's arm by one of the EMTs. I lay down on the concrete and gravel, facing the garage. The sun was setting and the tallest pine tree, the one Trent called Big Pine, was lit golden against the blue sky. It was beautiful and it made me happy that on his way out he got to see his favorite tree looking glorious.

38. Autopsy

September 19, 2008

The medical examiner called at a little after nine the next morning. Trent's parents had approved the autopsy, he said, and he would have the results later in the afternoon.

"This afternoon?"

"Yes."

I sat in a chair and Nemo sat by me. I had remembered to feed him but he didn't eat. I called two clients for whom I had work due and explained what had happened. They were kind and understanding. I didn't know it at the time, but they started a phone tree and called everyone they could think of who would care. I called my parents. They were both shocked and they both cried. My dad sounded shaken.

The medical examiner called at a little after one o'clock.

"I have the results of the autopsy."

I sat down. "You do?"

"Yes. And I can tell you that sometimes when we do an autopsy the cause of death is inconclusive. But most of the time it's obvious and this was one of those times."

"Okay."

"He had a dissection of the aorta, which is what we call it. A dissection is simply a fancy word for a tear. The aorta is—"

"I know what the aorta is."

"So he had a weak spot in his heart, and it tore. And when it tore, the pericardium, the sac that surrounds the heart, filled up with blood. The pressure of the blood on the heart made it impossible for his heart to beat."

I put his words together in my head, going back to anatomy class and the plastic model of the heart and imagining a tear on the inside.

"You're telling me he died of a broken heart."

"Yes! Precisely. That is exactly what we say."

I could tell that he was happy to have been understood. I had questions, though.

"Did it hurt him?"

"Well, he . . . he probably felt some initial discomfort but any pain wouldn't have lasted long. He would have died very quickly. His circulation was entirely shut down."

"I'm glad it didn't hurt."

"I can also tell you that it didn't matter what he was doing. He could have been chopping wood or sleeping in bed, it wouldn't have mattered. When the wall of the heart tears like that, it goes in its own time. It has nothing to do with exertion."

"Oh. That's interesting."

"Also, it wouldn't have mattered where it happened. Even if it had happened in the ER, nobody could have saved him—there is no way to make the blood circulate, and without circulation, there's no oxygen being delivered to the body."

"That's good to know. Thank you."

"You couldn't have saved him."

"Thank you."

I would need to tell Justin this.

Jenna and I spoke twice that day. The first time Doreen called and said that Jenna couldn't remember everything I had told her, and she wanted me to walk her though it again, which I did. The second time I called her to tell her about the autopsy results.

Trent's father called that afternoon and asked me to talk with Jean, because she was having a hard time believing her only son was dead. When she got on the phone, her "Hello" sounded woozy but I forged ahead.

"Hello, Jean."

"Is Trent really dead?"

"Yes, Jean, Trent is dead."

"Are you sure?"

"Yes, I'm sure. When I got home he was lying in the driveway and his face was blue. The emergency people came and tried to help him but they couldn't, and they took his body away in the ambulance."

"Are you sure it was him?"

"Yes. I did CPR on him. I'm sure."

"Oh. Okay. Good-bye."

I guess no mother wants to believe her son is dead. I guess believing it was some other body in the driveway was easier.

39. Arrangements

September 19, 2008

Steven became the go-between for the funeral arrangements. He was technically Trent's cousin, but since Steven's mother and Trent's mother are twins, Trent, Steven, and Steven's older brother Gary spent a lot of time together growing up. They were more like brothers, especially Gary and Trent. Steven may have taken on the role because of what happened on the phone, when Jean said good-bye and Herb got back on the phone.

"Thank you. Maybe that will help. We're both just so lost without Trent."

"I know what you did, Herb."

"What are you talking about?"

"I know how you hurt him."

"Everybody got hurt."

So Steven stepped in and coordinated the arrangements. Herb and Jean would arrange and pay for the funeral. I agreed because I knew I couldn't give Trent what he really wanted. What he wanted, what he had told me he wanted, was to have his body shot out of a cannon over the swamp at Mud Lake. I told Steven that the only thing I wanted at the funeral was to speak.

Because the death was unwitnessed, state law required that they hold the body in Muskegon for forty-eight hours. The funeral would be on Monday, September 22nd.

When Trent and I had moved to Newaygo, his life became a mystery to his friends. I wanted to clear it up. I wanted them to know how he had lived and how he died. I wanted to set the record straight, at least for the previous few years. If I could do nothing else for Trent, at least I could speak on his behalf.

September 21, 2008

Thank goodness for Denise, one of the friends on the bicycle ride that led me to leave the man in the purple suspenders. Denise is wise, wise about family dynamics and, unfortunately, wise about the politics of funerals. Denise carried me.

On Sunday, I drove to the cottage she and her husband had bought about fifteen years earlier. They had spent years replacing windows and building walls and a staircase and a second floor that looked over a small lake. The air was cool. Denise ferried me around the lake on their pontoon boat and we watched the sun sink into the trees. It got even cooler. We didn't talk much.

In the house Denise hugged me when I cried and was quiet most of the time. I couldn't really think about the funeral but that was okay because Denise thought for me, strategizing on my behalf.

"Do you want to see Trent's body?"

"What?"

"You might want to decide in advance whether you want to see Trent's body or not. That way, when we get to the church, I can take you to your seat in a way that, depending on what you want, will either allow you to see him or avoid it."

"Oh. Good idea."

Denise waited but I didn't speak again.

"Do you know what you want?"

I thought back to Lee's funeral. Lee was a school friend and roommate who died when she was twenty-five and I was twenty-four. She had been riding her bicycle, was late for work, and was trying to catch the tail end of a yellow light when she came head-to-grill with a delivery truck making a left-hand turn. The driver of the truck was seventeen.

Lee had been in the hospital, in a coma, for a week before her parents gave the word to stop the machines that were breathing for her. We had seen the X-ray of her brain—the blood flow went no higher than the lowest little part of her brain at the top of her neck. When they took her off life support, there were no breaths left.

Lee had two funerals. The first was in Minnesota, where we lived. The second was in New Jersey, where we were from. The first service was open casket, which was a mistake.

Lee was wearing a blue dress I had never seen her in—she wore only blue jeans or plaid skirts. The day of the accident she was wearing a long, pleated plaid skirt and because she was late for work she had not ironed it. I can still see her there, in our living room, moving quickly to gather her things in her wrinkled skirt, and me disapproving.

In the casket, to go with her dress, she wore two blue scarves. One was around her head to hide the fact that they had shaved her head when they did the surgery and one was around her neck, to hide the hole from the tracheotomy. The scarves looked all right, maybe a pattern that Lee would have liked, and I was glad because her mother had sent me out to buy them for this purpose.

I was looking at Lee when her father appeared, took my elbow, and walked me to a seat. He must have done that because I must have been standing there for a long time. I was looking at her face and trying to see the Lee I had known.

Her face had swollen from both the injury and the fluids pumped into her. When the wires and the tubes and the pumps were removed, her face shrunk like a deflated balloon, wrinkling and collapsing onto her bones. She could have passed for eighty.

They kept the casket closed in New Jersey.

Denise was waiting patiently as I thought all these things, as I calculated my answer—did I want to see Trent?

"No, I don't."

September 22, 2008

I did want to go by the casket, though, to put something in it. Denise and I also talked about the politics of where I would sit and whom I would ride with to the burial. I wanted to go with her but she said it would probably be better if I went with someone from the family. Steven called and suggested that I sit with him and his wife at the funeral and that I ride with them to the burial. He said that Herb and Jean had also said I was welcome to ride with them.

"I don't want to go with them. I want to go with you."

Denise drove me, on the back roads because she thought it would be prettier, to the church in Marshall, Michigan. She was right, it was prettier. The wheat fields were tall and golden in the early morning sun.

The church was crowded and we executed our plan to take me near the casket. We shuffled slowly through the crowd, as if we were going through a ticket gate for a show. When it became obvious that I wasn't going to look at Trent in his casket, someone said, loudly, "She should see the body. It would be good for her." I didn't see who spoke and I didn't want to. Instead I responded loudly into the air. "I saw him dead when he died."

We got close and I slipped the envelope into the casket, along the side. I could see Trent was in a green shirt but I didn't look any closer than that. I put my hand on his chest one last time, which was a mistake. The velour of the new shirt felt soft under my hand but underneath was hard, like a box, and I realized they must have put something in him to hold his chest up after the autopsy.

Whatever was in that box wasn't Trent.

Someone pulled me aside for a brief prayer with the family. We stood in a circle and held hands. I didn't want to be there. When the prayer was over, we hugged each other. I didn't want to do that, either.

40. Eulogy

September 22, 2008

I was in the second pew between Steven and his wife. They were newlyweds and I was grateful that they had separated themselves to surround me. The kindness meant a great deal.

The pastor stood and went to the podium. I remembered him from the last funeral Trent and I had attended at this church, the one when Trent told me he felt sorry for the woman's father but not for her husband. The pastor was wearing a long, shiny green robe and I wondered how they decide what color robe to wear.

The pastor paused, looked out at the crowd, and then spoke. "Trent Allen Price was a difficult child. He was a handful. He was trouble with a capital T." A few people chuckled. I didn't. I pressed my palms into the wooden bench to stop from screaming. Even now. Even at his funeral they could not honor their son.

He continued to speak and I wasn't sure who he was talking about or even who was talking. Sometimes he sounded like a pastor, sometimes he sounded like Jean. I decided that listening would only make me angry so I stopped. I simply sat there until his mouth stopped moving.

He then looked out over the crowd and asked whether anyone would like to speak. I stood up. I had already pulled my paper bag into my lap, the bag that held my props and my words. I walked to the front of the church. As I stepped over a wooden guardrail, I heard a few laughs and wondered whether I had just committed some sort of sacrilege. Oh well.

When I got to the podium, I turned to the pastor, who stood a few steps away.

"You might want to get comfortable," I told him. "This is going to take a while."

He chuckled and gave me a kind look. I looked back at him with level eyes.

"I'm not kidding."

I took my things out of the bag, placed them on the podium, and looked up to see that the church was crowded with people and they were wearing all kinds of attire. Some were in suits, the bikers were in leathers, hunters were in camo, others were in their best jeans. I was wearing a white turtleneck, a new red hooded sweatshirt that Trent had said I looked cute in, and my most comfortable jeans. I was dressed for Trent and for me and for no one else.

Because I tend to speak too softly when speaking to a group, I silently reminded myself to speak up. I unfolded my paper and looked at the words. They had come either the morning before or the morning before that and I had written them as they came to me. They came so easily that it was almost like taking notes while someone else was talking. I had typed them up and practiced saying them a couple of times. That was enough.

They were hard to read, though, because my hands were shaking. That surprised me. I laid the notes on the podium and pressed my palms down on either side of the notes, careful not to cover any of the words. Then I began.

> Trent Price hated funerals. He hated dressing up so he
> bought a pair of black jeans that he wore to funerals and
> to weddings. At funerals, he hated that people talked

about the person who had died as if they were perfect. So I will do my best to be even-handed.

After Trent moved to Newaygo, I think most people don't know what happened to him, so that's what I'm going to talk about. Let's start with how he died.

The medical examiner said Trent had a thin spot in the wall of his heart, in his aorta. The wall tore apart. For those of you in construction, it's like instead of a 2×4, somebody slipped in a piece of lath and it was weak and it broke. The blood flowed into the sac surrounding his heart and his heart couldn't beat. It wouldn't have mattered what he was doing—he could have been chopping wood or sleeping and it still would have happened when it happened. It didn't matter where he was—he could have been in the woods or in the ER. There was nothing anybody could have done to save him.

I looked at Justin when I said that part. I wanted Justin to know.

Now let's fill in the blanks after he moved from Mud Lake to Newaygo.

One of the first things that happened was that he got glasses. Now that he was driving roads he hadn't been driving his whole life, we both realized that he couldn't read the street signs. It turned out that he needed bifocals and he took very good care of them.

At this point, I took out my first prop, Trent's glasses. If Trent's mother was having trouble believing that Trent was dead, the glasses would help. When I said the part about Trent taking very good care of the glasses, I held them up for everyone to see—most of the glasses in one hand and one of the bows in the other. People laughed because they thought Trent had broken them. He hadn't.

When Trent died his glasses either fell off or he had already taken them off. They got stepped on by the emergency people and they broke. Trent was walking out of the barn and he just fell over, face up, facing the barn. The last thing he saw was the sky and the trees. At that time of day his favorite tree, the Big Pine, was lit up and glowing.

I seem to have reverted to how he died; let's go back to how he spent his time.

Trent took care of the house. He did a lot of building and fixing up. He insulated and sheathed the walls in the barn. He replaced the propane tank with one that was refurbished so it was better than new and cheaper than new, which was Trent's favorite kind of deal. He sealed the deck, rebuilt the bathroom floor, and together we painted Jenna's bedroom. He built me an office. He cut down seventeen trees to make a drive around the barn.

Trent's last outside project was for me. I told him I wanted to be able to see blue sky out the bedroom window and I thought four trees would need to be removed. The four trees turned into eleven. Trent didn't just cut the trees down, he pulled the stumps out and you can see them do it on Jeremy's Myspace page. When I was in Chicago, Trent had the area excavated.

He told me over the telephone that when I got home I would see how beautiful it was.

The day he died, Trent had picked up Justin to get some work done, had the house cleaned, had done some shopping—he bought a roast and bacon from the meat market and milk, apples, and orange juice from the grocery store. He had Justin mow the lawn—I think he was getting ready to leave because, as Steven reminded me recently, "Trent always did like to have the grass cut before he went out of town."

What else did Trent do since moving to Newaygo? He was a student at Baker College. He did okay in math and got a B–. In algebra he fought with his teacher when she said that a 20-foot ladder leaning against a wall was 23.3 feet up the wall. He said that was impossible. The teacher did the problem twice and came up with the same answer each time. With that Trent swore, left the room, and that was pretty much the end of algebra for him.

In English, he got an A. His teacher went to a conference and chose one of his papers to read as a sample of her students' work. Here's the surprise: Trent loved school. He liked learning and his face lit up when he talked about it. He loved it.

Trent also started making friends in Newaygo. Ed was first. Trent called him "Ed Mowin" because Ed makes his living from mowing lawns. Ed took Trent with his buddies when they went kayaking.

Trent met Gene when Gene plowed the driveway. Gene reminded Trent of his uncle O.T., and sometimes after visiting Gene, Trent would cry because Gene is old and has cancer.

Most recently, Trent spent time with Justin and Jeremy, whom he called the twins even though they aren't. They survived Trent's summer jobs program and became very close. The four of us went kayaking on the Muskegon a few weeks ago and had a nice time.

It was Justin who found Trent. Justin had been splitting wood, came to the front for a drink, and found Trent face up and blue in the driveway. Justin had the presence of mind to call 9-1-1 and then started CPR. Justin and his mom stayed until after all the medical people had left. I was glad they were there.

So Trent kayaked, he built things, he went to school. The best thing that happened in Newaygo was when Jenna moved in.

Trent loved cooking Jenna dippin' eggs on Saturdays and banana pancakes on Sundays. We played Sorry! and Rummikub—which Jenna won most of the time and it wasn't because we let her. Trent and Jenna had a few big fights and a couple times he swore at her.

Once I asked Trent what he wanted most for Jenna. "I want her to be strong, to be able to take care of herself," he told me. Well, baby, you can quit now, because you got that.

We read together. Trent didn't read well; the words got jumbled up in his head and it was hard for him to follow what was happening. I thought he might have dyslexia but he refused to get it checked. So we read together in bed at night. His favorite book of all time was *Endurance*—the story of the explorer Ernest Shackleton.

I held up the book so people could see it.

An unopened box at home was delivered when I was in Chicago—it has the next two books we were going to read.

Trent didn't read well but he was a poet. One time he wrote, "Our bones and our flesh will be gone and we'll still be loving each other." And that's what I think Trent is doing right now. I think he's loving us.

After I sat down again in the pew, Jenna stood up and went to the podium. She spoke from paper, and I was impressed with what she said and how she said it. Trent had wanted her to be strong. Here was proof.

Jenna then showed a video she had made, for the wake and for the funeral. It had photos of her dad, set to music, with words interspersed. Other people told me one of their favorite photos was of Jenna as a baby, lying on Trent's chest, all curled up and small in his arms.

I have two favorite photos from the video. One is of Jenna and Trent when Jenna was eight. They are in their bathing suits, standing in front of the used pop-up trailer that Trent had bought for the summer just so he could take Jenna swimming in lakes and have a convenient place to stay. They are standing side by side, shoulders back, bellies out, tanned and a bit burned, big grins stretched across their faces.

The other picture isn't of Trent, but of his feet. Or rather, of the marks his feet left on the snow on the back deck. Jenna was smart enough in the video to leave the photo up long enough for most people to figure out what Trent was doing when his feet made those marks. They laughed.

So many people were at the church that the line for food snaked around the outer edges of the room. Someone told me it would be okay if I cut in front, so I did, which is a good thing because the church ran out of food and chairs.

A friend was at the church with her two children, who thought Trent must have really liked Jell-O because there were so many different colors. They were too young to understand the economics of feeding a crowd.

My friend's daughter was happy to see me and, because she was young enough not to know that you are supposed to be sad at funerals, jumped into my arms when she spotted me. It felt so good to be holding this happy small person that I didn't want to put her back down.

Later, when Herb and Jean were greeting people, Herb started to hug me. I stopped him.

"I already hugged you once. I'm not doing it again."

When the body was loaded into the hearse, I saw that one of the pallbearers was Dick. I wanted to scream. Dick had killed the piebald. I wanted to run up and pull him from the casket and say, "You have no right!" but I just stood there.

At the burial, Trent's cousin Jimo* told me that now that Trent was gone, I would need a tall fence and a security system installed. He would be happy to do it, he said, out of respect for Trent. I didn't want either a fence or a security system but had to find a way to tell Jimo without offending him or hurting his feelings.

Steven was standing with us and gave me a look that said, *If you want, I'll lead him away from here*, because Jimo is a bit odd. But I knew what to say. The best way to talk to a person who thinks differently is to talk in accordance with how they think.

"I know you want me to be safe, and I want to be safe, but you don't have to worry about installing a security system or a fence because the spirits of the Indians that used to live on our land will protect me and keep me safe."

Jimo was doubtful at first but then he agreed. Steven gave me a bit of a wink over how well my approach had worked.

What Steven didn't know is that I believed in the Indians. One night in Newaygo, as I was drifting off to sleep, I heard drumming. Not the slow *dum-da-dum-dum* that you hear in the movies, but much faster. I asked Trent whether he had heard them. He had.

Meanwhile, Denise was trying to help me find a way to remember the location of the plot. She pointed out trees and buildings beyond the wrought iron fence as navigation aids. I tried to remember based on the trees, but there were just too many of them.

After the burial, different people walked up to say they were sorry. The number of people was shrinking, though, and finally I thought I was talking with the very last person. I then noticed an older man a little distance away, not talking to any of the family, not talking to anyone. He was neatly dressed and had that graying at the temples that often makes men look distinguished. By the cut of his blazer and the way the cloth of his slacks ruffled in the small breeze, I knew he wasn't from Battle Creek. He was a well-to-do stranger and he was waiting for me.

I ended the conversation and walked toward him. He moved toward me and extended his hand.

"Hi, I'm Joel—"

Joel! This was Trent's uncle, his father's brother, the one who had moved to Colorado, the one Trent had talked about going to visit. Trent thought Joel could help him understand his father; he thought Joel had an important story to tell. All this came quickly to mind before Joel finished his introduction.

"—and I'm the black sheep of the family."

"Not to me, you're not."

We hugged and I thought he was built more like Trent than his brother—bigger, but not as big as Trent. As we hugged he spoke very softly.

"I'm afraid of my brother."

I said the only words that came to mind.

"For good reason."

41. Coming to Terms

Telling Ernest

I wanted to tell Ernest that Trent was dead, so I walked down to the swamp along the two-track that went through the woods until it got lost in the sand hill that bottomed out at the swamp lake. I didn't even know whether Ernest was still alive, but if he was, I wanted him to know.

"Ernest."

It was stupid to think Ernest would be there or that he would hear me. Or that he would know who I was. But I called him again, anyway.

"Ernest."

The orange-striped head of a painted turtle popped up out of the water. My feet were in the grass, inches from the edge of the water, and Ernest was an equal number of inches on the other side.

We looked at each other for a minute or two. I just wanted to look at him, I was so happy to see him again. Then I told him.

"Trent's dead."

Ernest looked at me for a few seconds. His reaction was just like everybody else's. He didn't believe it at first. He blinked and looked at me but I wasn't going to say it again, the way I did with people when they said, "What?" and I told them again and then they said, "What?" again. Most people had to be told three times.

Ernest needed to hear it only once. He blinked a few more times. Then he went back under the water and I walked back up the sand hill to home.

Dancing

I was facing my regrets. One was that I had never danced with Trent. He had asked me once and I had declined. It seemed the nice thing to do because he had told me he didn't enjoy it and definitely not in public. Instead, I'd danced with the man celebrating his twenty-fifth wedding anniversary. I learned the celebrating man was lecherous and for the first time saw Trent so angry that he left the room.

After Trent died and the lecherous man came by to comfort me, I sent him away. He sent his wife over and I told her she was welcome any time but that her husband was not. Trent had thought the lecherous man beat his wife. She did have the look of a beaten dog.

Feeling this regret and this loss, one night in bed I spoke words into the air I hoped Trent could hear. I told him I was sorry I hadn't danced with him and asked if I could in my dreams.

Nothing happened. The next night I asked again and again nothing happened. The third night I asked again, saying that I would never ask again and could I please dance with him in my dreams just this once.

We did dance that night but in a different way. We danced through the solar system, dancing up and over and around stars and planets, flying through a very black sky. We moved quickly but easily and gracefully.

Because we didn't really have bodies our clothes weren't quite like real clothes. They were made of nothing, as if smoke had been pressed together. Trent wore a soft, black tuxedo and a blue shirt that matched my dress. If we had been in a room, my dress would have filled it.

We danced and flew for hours and it was wonderful to be with him in such an amazing way. When I woke up my teeth were vibrating.

It was my first and last dance with him and it was amazing.

Overdraft

The pump at the gas station wouldn't authorize my debit card and I was pretty sure what the problem was. I hadn't been paying attention to my checkbook, though for most of my life I had generally been careful about keeping good accounts. When Trent first told me that Doreen wouldn't let him near their checkbook, I decided that he and I would balance ours together. Now, I didn't want to do it without him.

Arm Sweater

A couple of weeks after Trent died, I slowly realized that my arms didn't feel the same. The left arm felt as if it were wearing a sweater, not on the whole arm, just on the top of the arm, from my wrist to just shy of my shoulder.

It was odd, but I thought back to some nights previously, when I had asked Trent for a way to know that he was still there. Trent had slept to my left. When we lay side by side, my left arm was bathed in the curly warm hairs of his right arm. It was as if the top of my arm was wearing a sweater. The arm sweater feeling stayed in place until the afternoon I picked up Nemo from our friend Joe's house, where Nemo had been staying while I was in Chicago. Trent would have been happy that Joe's huskies had taught Nemo to pee like a boy.

I was on M-82, happy to be back in in Newaygo and happy to be with Nemo. Then, suddenly, the arm sweater disappeared.

I screamed, "I can't feel you anymore!"

As the last word came out of my mouth, the car—I had taken Trent's Altima rather than my Jeep—lost power, dropping from 60 to 20.

"Okay," I said aloud. "You're still here. Please don't let the car die and please get me home."

I was able to get the car to go 30 and that's how I drove the remaining six miles, glad to be rolling and really glad when we pulled into the driveway.

The mechanic could find nothing wrong with the Altima. It was working fine but the arm sweater was gone, permanently. A few months after that, Nemo was also gone. My friends knew the condition Trent had so emphatically laid out and were determined to help me honor it. My friend Debbi found a home for Nemo with her nephew and his wife, in the suburbs of Chicago in a nice house with a big fenced yard and two kids who wrap their arms around him like a giant teddy bear.

42. Belongings

October–November 2008

"I want everything that was O.T.'s."

Trent's mother was throwing me for a loop again. This time, instead of being hazy and struggling to believe that her son was dead, she was present and pugnacious. She didn't start with "Hello." She started with what she wanted.

"Anything that was O.T.'s, I want it."

"I understand, Jean."

"He was my uncle. He was my Uncle O.T."

"Yes. Trent told me."

"I want Steven to have his guns."

"Okay."

"All his guns. I want Steven to have all O.T.'s guns."

"Yes, Steven gets all O.T.'s guns," and I wondered how many guns there were. I only knew about the one in the photo.

Jean kept on. "Steven gets all O.T.'s guns but I want everything else."

"I'll pull out everything that I know was O.T.'s and put it all together so it's easy to find."

"Good."

"What about the photographs?"

"What?"

"The two photos of O.T. that Steven took. One's a close-up. In the other he's sitting in a rocking chair, holding a shotgun."

"I don't want those. Steven already gave me those."

"What about Trent's clothes? Do you want any of those?"

"What would I want those for?"

We discussed when they were coming. It would be on a Saturday. Jean and Herb were coming with Trent's sister; Steven and his wife were coming. Jenna would come with her grandparents. That's when I pushed back.

"Jean, I want Jenna to go first."

"What?"

"When you go through the house for what you want, I want Jenna to go first. Alone."

"I'm his mother."

"Yes. And Jenna is his daughter. Don't you think Trent would want his daughter to have what she wanted that was his?"

Trent's mother gave in more easily than I thought she would but it didn't matter. I knew what Trent would have wanted and I was going to fight for it if I had to. My plan was simple. I called Jenna to explain.

"Jenna, when you get here on Saturday, you're going to go into the house first. I'm going to give you blue tape and you get to put the blue tape on everything you want. That way, when other people come in after you they'll know what you want and leave it alone."

"Can I have the bed?"

"Oh, Jenna, I should have said anything you want that was your dad's. The bed was mine and I want to sleep in it again."

"Yeah, I knew it was. Okay."

I didn't tell her that although I spoke in the future tense, the truth was past tense. After the ambulance left, I had never slept in the upstairs bed again.

Jenna and I talked some more. It was hard for me not to feel sorry for her. I remembered what had happened in my grandmother's house after she had died, and I had a pretty good idea this would be worse.

First Dibs

Later I called Jenna again. I wanted to be sure I knew which of Trent's things she wanted. I wanted her to have first dibs on everything. She wanted the big clock, and the old-fashioned cabinet that held the stereo and the television, and the picnic table. She wanted the three framed black-and-white photographs Steven had taken of Trent and Jenna, when Jenna was eight or so. She wanted one of the three-wheelers.

I then asked whether she wanted any of Trent's clothes. "I want his sweatshirt." Trent had several sweatshirts, but when she spoke in the singular, I knew exactly which one she meant—the camouflage one. It was his favorite, and he wore it almost daily in cooler weather, the layer that went between his T-shirt and his khaki Carhartt vest. It was the sweatshirt he had been wearing when he pulled two cold beers from the kangaroo pocket the night we navigated our responses to the note I had left him.

"Can you make me a pillow out of his T-shirts?" she asked me. "A great big pillow with a big red heart on one side?"

If she and I had been talking face to face, I would have scooped her up in my arms and hugged her and told her I was sorry.

"Yes, Jenna, I can make you a great big pillow."

Hiding

Elaine and the close friends I asked all said the same thing: "Hide what you want."

It didn't seem right to me. It seemed deceitful. But I thought about Elaine's advice, back when I confessed that I had lied to get away from the man in the purple suspenders. Elaine has relatives who are alive through deceit, which has contributed to her perspective. Her philosophy is that people must earn your truth. I thought about Trent's parents and asked myself whether they had earned my truth. They had not.

First I took things for Jenna, following the same rule for myself that I had given to Jean: "Jenna gets what she wants first."

I was happy that Jenna wanted the camo sweatshirt. Suddenly I had a plan. I had three heavy Chiquita banana boxes and would fill them for Jenna. The day before Jenna and Trent's parents and the others came to pick up Trent's things, I put them in my office and locked the door.

For myself . . .

> one of the four wool blankets that had belonged to O.T., all of which I had rescued from the back of the barn and cleaned early on (this violated Jean's request and I didn't care)
>
> the Carhartt sweatshirt
>
> his bow and the smaller bow Trent had said was mine
>
> the carp target
>
> five pieces of pottery he had made
>
> a wooden letter holder he had made in high school shop class
>
> three wooden fish
>
> his kayaking paddle and mine
>
> his life vest and mine
>
> three of his four books (cooking wild game, finding edible mushrooms, and shooting carp), leaving behind the history of Barry County, Michigan

The upstairs loft in the Newaygo house had a small door that opened to a small space beneath the rafters. The door was hidden by the bookcase Trent had built for me. I put all these things in that space behind the door. I then took our wedding rings and tucked them in the back corner of my underwear drawer.

Last, I took Trent's duffel bag and packed it for Steven. Inside went the red plaid hunting coat and an old wooden hunting knife with a compass on the end. The knife might have belonged to O.T. but I didn't know. Again, a potential violation of Jean's request and again I didn't care.

When I was finished, I was exhausted and a little paranoid and very fragile.

A Test

The items in the three banana boxes in the downstairs office and behind the little door to the attic space and in the duffel bag in the back of the Jeep began to bother me. It seemed wrong to hide them. Doubts scratched at me. I wrestled with this conflict until an idea came to me. I thought it was brilliant. It would confirm whether it had been right or unnecessary to hide things. It would be a lagging rather than a leading indicator, but it would be a true one.

The two photographs of O.T. hung in our living room in Newaygo, the close-up near the fireplace and the one with the shotgun next to the kitchen. We kept a framed photo of Trent's parents, a 2005 Christmas gift, in the hall closet where it would be ready for a visit from them. We had needed to take it out of the closet only once.

I took my favorite photo of O.T., the one with the gun, and put it in the little attic space. The photo of Trent's parents went on the nail where the photo of O.T. had been. Jean had said she didn't want the photos of O.T. because she already had them.

Time would tell.

Reinforcements

"Justin, can you and Jeremy work this Saturday?"

"No problem. What d'you want done?"

"The coop. The siding needs to be finished."

"Yep."

Justin had adopted Trent's way of saying "yep." They both said it as a two-syllable word, "yeah-up." Hearing Justin say it that way made me happy and sad at the same time.

"Justin, it's more than just the coop. Trent's parents are coming to get his stuff and I don't want to be alone."

"Uh-huh."

"I want you guys to use the chop saw and whatever other tools you'll need to finish the job so they don't take them."

"No problem."

"Justin?"

"Yeah?"

"This isn't going to be fun."

"No problem."

"I'll pick you and Jeremy up at eight o'clock."

"'K."

"Trent's parents are coming at nine. Jenna's coming, too."

"Jenna's coming?"

"Yes, she is."

Justin paused. Whatever it was he was wondering, his next question was tactical.

"How long you think they'll be there?"

"I don't know. But however long it is, you guys are getting paid for a whole day. You'll have earned it."

"No problem."

"Justin?"

"Yeah?"

"Thank you."

"No problem."

43. Armada

November 8, 2008

Justin and Jeremy came out the side door of their house, jeans and jackets loose on their lanky bodies, arms moving as if they were connected with marionette strings. They took their standard places in the Jeep—Justin up front and Jeremy in the back, sitting behind Justin. Justin looked like he had been crying but I wasn't sure. Jeremy was tapping on his cell phone, his soft, straight blond hair shielding his face. I couldn't see his eyes. They spoke in turns.

"I've got Trent's socks on."

"Me too."

"They're the warmest socks I've ever had."

"Yeah, we both wear them all the time."

When I had gone through Trent's dresser, I was surprised to find three never-worn pairs of his Redhead socks. I gave them to Justin, not sure whether he or his brother would want them. As usual, I had underestimated their level of need.

The boys quickly set up the equipment to work on the coop. It wasn't long before sawdust was spewing from the table saw. I couldn't think of anything for me to do so I went inside.

At nine o'clock, a truck pulled into the driveway. I was shocked at how large it was. The top of the truck hit the pine branches that spanned the driveway and broke off a few. I had pictured an average-size U-Haul. This one looked like a semi and pulled through the circular extension Trent had built on the driveway, stopping behind the barn. A car I didn't recognize was behind it and stopped in front of the garage. Another car was behind it. People got out of all the vehicles at the same time. There were more people than I had expected.

Trent's parents and Trent's sister I had expected, but not her husband, Kris. Steven I was glad for, but his wife was not there. I could understand why she would stay away but I missed her. Jean's sister was there. I hadn't expected her, which was stupid, because the twins attended all important events together. I did not see Jenna and panicked until suddenly she appeared.

Blue Tape

Jenna and I did not hug. I rarely hugged her in front of other people because I didn't know whether it would bother them, whether they would tell Doreen, and whether it would bother her. I walked Jenna across the grass and up the front steps, asking God or the universe or someone to help us both. I handed the blue tape to her and reminded her that the plan was for her to put blue tape on anything that was her dad's that she wanted.

As we walked through the front door, Jenna turned to me, eyes wide.

"There's already blue tape on things!"

"It's okay, Jenna. I already taped things I was pretty sure you would want."

"You did?"

"Yeah. But we can pull it off if there's anything I taped that you don't want."

"Oh. Okay."

Jenna stood in the living room and looked around. There was tape on the tall wooden wind-up clock, the stereo cabinet, and the television. The television was especially important because this was where Trent and Jenna had watched the home movies they made together. *The Blair Witch Project* was the first. A more complex murder mystery followed, for which I allowed ketchup to be smeared across the back of my shirt. Trent's friend Jimmy was the killer so that Trent could focus on filming. We had given Jimmy a large butcher knife as a prop, but Jimmy wasn't very scary because during the scene where he is supposed to be sneaking in the back door, the first thing Jimmy did was wipe his shoes on the mat. Trent named it *The Case of the Courteous Killer*.

The last one was simple, Jenna and Trent dancing to Chris Brown's "Kiss Kiss." The video features a straw cowboy hat which they take turns stealing from each other and then dancing a hat-ownership victory dance. This was the video that Trent wanted to watch again a couple of weeks before he died but the camera battery was dead. I had searched Jenna's closet several times but couldn't find the adapter. It turned up later under a stack of clothes and stuffed animals in the back corner of Jenna's closet, in a place I had checked at least twice but somehow missed. When I found it, I cried.

Jenna took the roll of blue tape and began marking what she wanted. She wasn't greedy. She was thoughtful. She was precise. We slowly walked the whole house until we were both sure she had everything she wanted.

As we left the house and walked to the garage, I was glad at how well our time inside the house had gone. Neither of us had cried. Jenna asked a few questions and marked what she wanted. I was surprised at how thoughtfully and quickly she had worked.

We opened the garage door to chaos. The first thing I noticed was that my gardening tools were no longer hanging on the wall. Jenna turned to me, eyes wide, pained.

"I need my blue tape!"

"We'll get it. It's going to be okay."

I then addressed everyone. "Where are my gardening tools?"

"They're in the truck." This was Jean.

"But they're mine."

"They're already in the truck. In the front, behind other things."

"We'll get them," Steven said. "We didn't know they were yours."

Jenna wailed. "I need my blue tape!"

Steven managed to pause the action. I had thought that the family would have been patiently waiting while Jenna and I were in the house. I was wrong.

We agreed that someone would find and unload my gardening tools. I had told the family that I only wanted the things the boys and I would need to maintain the house until it sold—the saws, the snow blower—but it never occurred to me that they would assume that everything in the garage was Trent's. Steven asked me to point out what was mine.

We decided also that the family would go into the house while Jenna stayed in the garage and marked what she wanted with the blue tape. She taped Trent's tall captain's chair, the Winchester stool, and the Budweiser sign that said, "Hunters Welcome." I don't know what else she marked because I went back into the house to see how things were going there.

All I remember is that I felt naked, as if the life that Trent and I—and for a little while, Jenna—had lived was being fingered and appraised and taken or not.

When I went down to the basement, I noticed my sewing kit open on the floor, bobbins spewed across the concrete, their skinny thread tails marking their path. Jean pointed to a white crocheted bedspread in a clear vinyl case and asked me if I wanted it. "That was my grandmother's," I told her abruptly.

I floated between the house and the garage, not knowing where to be, not wanting to be there, wanting to be everywhere. It felt as if everything was wrong but I couldn't figure out exactly what was wrong. I looked at what Jean had given me when they first arrived—the remains of the flowers that Anne and Dean had sent to Trent's funeral a month earlier. The basket and pinecones were still in good shape, but the flowers had wilted and stiffened and blackened.

"This is for you," Jean said as she handed it to me. "I was going to give it to you when you came to our house after the funeral but you never showed up."

I knew something wasn't right about those dead flowers but I couldn't figure out what. I took the basket and set it on the porch. I couldn't or wouldn't bring it into the house. That was the only thing I was sure of. That and blue tape.

Shell Shocked

"Do you want to have one of the guns? To protect yourself?"

Steven was asking and it was so hard to answer.

"I don't like guns. But I think Trent would want me to have one."

"I think so, too."

I looked around at all the trees and wondered about danger, about who or what might come out of the woods now that Trent wasn't there. We were standing on the porch. I didn't know what words should come next. I didn't want a gun. I wanted wings. I wanted to fly, to float, to forget.

"There's a smaller handgun you'll be able to handle."

"A handgun?"

What flashed in my mind was the big handgun, the one with the wooden handle, the one that looked like the one Clint Eastwood used in *Dirty Harry,* the one that came out when Trent was looking for a way out.

"It's light. Small. You'll be okay with it."

I continued to watch Steven's mouth move. His words hit my ears but what I was interested in was his eyes. I wanted to see something that would tell me everything would be okay. His eyes revealed care and gentleness but no assurances.

"We won't leave until you know how to use it."

"Okay."

"Kris will teach you. He was in the military."

"Okay."

We moved to the side porch and a man I hardly knew showed me how to load the clip with bullets, how to put the clip in the gun, how to take the safety off, how to shoot it, how to unload it. When I had worked the bullets and the clip and the shooting enough to satisfy Kris, he said that was enough for today but that I had to keep practicing and that I should practice again tomorrow.

It was ending. Before they got back in the cars and truck and drove away, we talked about Jenna coming back with her mother to pick up the Altima and Trent's parents coming back with a pickup truck with a hitch to take the trailer with the kayaks and the canoes.

We talked about three-wheelers and the pig roaster at Jimo's they didn't know about. I think I hugged Jenna good-bye because I needed to and I didn't care whether it bothered anybody. I may have hugged other people good-bye as well, but I don't remember because I had left my body by then.

I was floating.

Vindication

When they were gone, when I knew it was safe, I came back into my body. I was standing in the front yard, on the patchy grass that never grew well because of the sandy soil. Brown oak leaves and yellow and orange maple leaves lay on the ground by my feet. The oak leaves were both pointy (red oak) and rounded (white oak). It was fall.

I didn't hear the saws anymore and I walked into the garage. Jeremy was coiling an extension cord; Justin was sweeping the concrete floor with the push broom.

It looked strange. So much was gone but so much was left. Trent saved everything.

Justin would never tell you how he felt but you could tell by watching him. His face was red, his head was down, and he slapped the floor with every stroke of the push broom.

"You okay?"

"Yeah."

"You don't look okay. You look angry."

Justin continued to sweep but the dam broke and his words poured out hot and fast.

"They treated it—they acted like this was a fucking garage sale and everything was free."

"They did."

"And they fucked you over."

"Is that what you think? You think they fucked me over?"

"They did. They fucked you over." He spat the words.

And I came back fast at him with mine. "So tell me—where is Trent's paddle? Or mine? Where is his life vest? You see them anywhere? Where is his bow—do they have that?"

Justin stopped slapping the floor with the broom and looked at me, his fine blond hair falling into his eyes. What I saw there was not anger but hurt.

"Justin, they didn't get a thing I didn't want them to have."

He looked at me and didn't say anything. I don't know if he believed it. But I did. Even though I was damaged, I did. I thought back to that moment not too long before they left, as I stood on the front lawn in the thin grass and Jean walked out of the house, my house, toward me. She had something in her right hand. She held it up so I could see it. It was the framed picture of O.T.

"Honey, do you mind if I take this?"

The smile started slowly from the corners of my mouth and grew strong, a smile not of joy but of vindication.

"Not at all, Jean. Go ahead. Take it."

I did practice shooting. I took a tall metal chair and put it in the backyard. I took the framed photograph of Herb and Jean and put it on the chair. I shot without emotion, but after shooting a few clips, I did enjoy seeing where the bullets had left their holes.

The End of Stuff

At some point, Trent's parents came back in a truck with a hitch for the trailer and the load it carried—the two canoes and the five kayaks. I pulled into the driveway one day and they were gone.

His parents came back another time to see if they wanted anything else. This time I was on the porch and Jean was below me, on the grass. She skipped the usual "Hello."

"Where are Trent's saws?"

"Steven has them."

"Those boys were using them when we were here before."

"Yes, but Steven has them now."

"Did Steven come back to get them?"

"Yes, he did."

"Oh. Well, where is Trent's bow? Where's that?"

"I sent it to Shannon."

"Glenn said he wanted it."

"Well, I think Trent would rather Shannon have it."

"But Glenn told me he wanted it. He and Trent used to go carp shooting together all the time."

"Glenn and Trent weren't exactly on speaking terms when Trent died."

"Oh. I didn't know that."

Later on, because Trent loved garage sales, I held a garage sale to get rid of the rest of it. Justin had advised that the sale happen shortly after April 15th, when people had their tax refunds but before they had spent them. The sale would be one day only because I knew I couldn't hold myself together for more than that.

Friday, April 17th, was a beautiful, sunny day, the first really warm day of the year. I took that as a gift from Trent. Even though we lived at the end of a dirt road in a hard-to-find spot, the driveway filled with cars as neighbors discovered great deals and called their friends.

"How much is this?" a man asked about an item on one of the metal shelves from Ralston.

"Oh, that's the ten-dollar shelf."

"You mean each of these things is ten dollars?"

"No, I mean everything on the shelf is ten dollars."

Because I wasn't clear or he didn't believe me, I repeated myself.

"You can have that whole shelf, everything on it, for ten dollars."

Moments like that were fun. Others weren't, like when the woman asked if I thought the airbed that Trent and I had slept on when we went camping would work as a pool float. Justin had to run an extension cord so the woman could inflate the bed to be sure it didn't have any leaks. It looked wrong inflated on the concrete in front of the garage. It belonged in a tent, or in the back of Trent's van. It belonged in the woods of northern Michigan, not in somebody's swimming pool.

When the garage sale was over I hid most of the money inside a stuffed animal. Then I took some of it and walked to Linda's Hit the Road Joe, a coffee shop a mile away that also sold artwork, and bought myself an angel.

44. Interlude

In November of 2008, I put money down on a to-be-built condo in the suburbs of Chicago. In the spring of 2009, I put our Newaygo house up for sale. When Trent and I first moved in, I had told him, "This house is no good for me without you." Even so, I briefly thought about trying to keep it, until the Friday night when I came back from being in Chicago and saw that someone had stolen our firewood. The next morning I walked the yard to see whether anything else was missing.

Trent had saved the largest pine trees that he had cut down because he wanted to build a cabin out of them. There were eleven or twelve of them, stacked a little ways back in the woods, on the edge of the clearing where the cabin was to be built. They were gone. It would have been possible to think they had never been there, except for a few small pyramids of fresh pine sawdust on the ground. The thieves must have been there for days.

I had to sell the house and I did, for much less than I paid for it, because it was 2009 and that's what it took to sell it. I understand about sunk costs.

I moved into an apartment, taking a month-to-month lease until the condo was completed, which was expected to be in June. More than a year later, in August of 2010, I walked away from the unfinished condo and my down payment.

I was still living in the apartment. And I was sad.

45. Clinging

August 17, 2010

I have been clinging to grief. I have been clinging to grief in a perverse way of feeling better. If I hurt this much, I must have really loved him. If I hurt this much, he must have really loved me.

What caused me to realize this was a blog post. The solution came from a movie. I would prefer to say I reached this enlightenment through meditation or contemplation of spiritual writings, but I take my lessons where they come.

The idea that I have willingly been choosing to walk into grief came from one of Seth Godin's blog posts.

> Occasionally we encounter emotions at random. More often, we have no choice, because there's something that needs to be done, or an event that impinges itself on us. But most often, we seek

emotions out, find refuge in them, just as we walk into the living room or the den.

Stop for a second and reread that sentence, because it's certainly controversial. I'm arguing that more often than not, we encounter fear or aggravation or delight because we seek it out, not because it's thrust on us.

Seth was right. In this situation, in this life of mine, I was choosing to walk into the grief room. I was like a six-year-old who has lost a tooth and probes the hole with her tongue, in doing so expanding the pain, and because of the nature of the innervation of the tongue, expanding the apparent size of the hole, and when continuing to probe the hole in a protracted manner, expanding the time it takes to heal. I have been that six-year-old, probing my wound, running my tongue over the edges of my grief. I have taken perverse pleasure from the pain of feeling the hole.

Last weekend, I drove to the shores of Lake Michigan to go to the party of a woman I had met at a conference. The event was the opening of the movie *Eat Pray Love*, a perfect chick flick. We wore bindis to the movie and smiled back at the people who smiled at us. Actually, we smiled at everyone.

When I read the book, I was ambivalent about Elizabeth Gilbert's husband, but in the movie I did not like him at all. *Let go*, I thought. *Why won't you let go of her?* And then I realized that he was me and the person I would not let go of, running after him, dangling from his angel wings, was Trent.

"But I still love you."

"So love me."

"But I miss you."

"So miss me. Send me love and light every time you think of me, then drop it."

I decided to take Elizabeth Gilbert's advice. I will still love Trent. I will still miss him. And every time I think of Trent, I will send him light and love, then drop it.

46. Letting Go

January 16, 2011

Last Sunday, I took Trent's small handgun to the local police station. I went on a Sunday morning because although I have never been to a police station before, I figured it would be a quiet time. A woman wearing thick glasses was helping a man ahead of me. When he left, she smiled in a friendly way that surprised me.

I wanted to turn in a gun, I told her. She then picked up the phone and called someone who, judging from her responses, told her to call someone else. She called someone else. Then she told me to take a seat and that an officer would be out to see me in a few minutes.

The policeman who came to see me was young, smooth skinned, and shorter than me. He took me into a small room and we sat down. I set the gun case on the table in front of me. Children who grow up in homes where the actions of their parents are hurtful, random, and arbitrary learn to be wary of authority. So even though this smooth-skinned police officer seemed nice, I was wary and quiet.

"The clerk said you would like to turn in a gun."

"Yes."

"Is this it?"

"Yes."

"Where did you get it?"

"It was my boyfriend's. He died two years ago."

"You don't want to keep it?"

"No. I haven't shot it in a long time and it's dangerous for me to have it. I don't want it."

Walking out of the police station, I cried. Not over the gun. It had meant nothing to Trent and therefore meant nothing to me. I was crying over a different gun and a bullet in a ceiling and because some wounds just don't heal.

June 30, 2011

"Suicidal." Elaine used the word not the last time I saw her, but the time before that. She was referring to Trent. She had never used that word before and the label hit me hard. It was a professional diagnosis. A clinical category. A code on an intake form.

I had always said, "Trent wanted to kill himself," as if describing it in those words put it in the same category as "Trent wanted to take a walk" or some other innocuous activity. After he died, maybe several months later, I told Elaine that he had wanted to kill himself. It was a secret I could no longer carry alone. I was surprised that she wasn't surprised, that she already knew. Trent had told her.

I had wondered, a little, what Trent and Elaine talked about when he saw her alone. We would do that, sometimes. One of us would go in first for some alone time with Elaine. I always thought they were talking about Jenna. I'm sure they did that. But they also talked about death and wanting death. When Elaine used the word, she was explaining to me how in some ways it got worse for Trent in Newaygo. Yes, he was happy to be with me and happy to be living there, but he still carried a relentless pain. What was so difficult for him was that even though he had gotten, in a way, to heaven, the hell he had known was still there. What made him suicidal was knowing that the pain was never going to go away. He would hurt forever.

When Elaine spoke about this, she curled her left arm by her ribs and curled her hand inward, as if she were carrying something, like a football, but her hand was contracted as if in pain. She was trying to help me understand the physicality of Trent's suffering, as if it were a growth from a wound in his side, heavy and malignant.

November 26, 2011

In the waiting room of Elaine's office, between the big basket of chocolates and the water jug that dispenses cold and hot water, is a tall bookshelf crammed with books in no particular order. There are books on infertility and loss and body image. There are the poems of Rilke and Neruda. Elaine's doctoral dissertation is on the bottom shelf. It is a thick, black leather-bound book and I have read most of it, back when I first started seeing Elaine and was trying to determine whether she was a good therapist or a mediocre one. It told me that Elaine is very smart.

Sometimes when I look at Elaine's bookshelf there will be a book that seems to stick out a bit from the rest and say to me, "Hey! Look here!" This happened when I saw Elaine the time before last. The book was *No Death, No Fear,* by Thich

Nhat Hanh. I sat in the waiting room, quickly flipped to the chapter titled "Transforming Grief and Fear," and read this:

> On a beautiful sunny day, you look up into the sky and see a nice, puffy cloud floating through. You admire its shape, the way the light falls upon its many folds and the shadow it casts on the green field. You fall in love with this cloud. You want it to stay with you and keep you happy. But then the shape and color change. More clouds join with it, the sky becomes dark, and it begins to rain. The cloud is no longer apparent to you. It has become rain. You begin to cry for the return of your beloved cloud.
>
> You would not cry if you knew that by looking deeply into the rain you would still see the cloud.

When I walked into Elaine's office for my appointment, I brought the book in with me and we talked about where I can see Trent now that he no longer is what he was. I believe this. I believe that we do not die. I believe this not because of a religious upbringing (which I did not have) but because of eighth-grade science class, where we learned that energy cannot be created or destroyed.

Here is my logic from eighth grade, which I still hold:

> People are energy. Proof: if you sit in a chair recently vacated by someone else, the chair will feel hot. If people make their own heat they must have their own energy.
>
> If you put a dead person in a chair, the dead body will not make the chair hot. But, when the dead body was alive, it would have made the chair hot. Therefore, the energy must have gone

somewhere, since it can be neither created nor destroyed.

Because energy cannot be destroyed, Trent's energy must be somewhere. If he is no longer the cloud, he is the rain. If he is no longer the beating heart, he is the sun. If he is no longer the hand that holds mine, he is the stars.

January 24, 2012

When I saw Elaine last Saturday, before sitting on her soft leather couch, I picked up the big cotton quilt from her rocking chair. It might be Mexican but I don't know. The colors are very bright. We both sat on the couch, each at one end and turned toward the other. At some point, as we talked through the list I had brought, Elaine set a box of Kleenex next to me. Never mind that there was a box on the table right behind me.

We were close to finished but there was still time left in the hour. I drew the quilt up under my chin, remembering something I had wanted to talk about.

"I don't know how long I could have lasted, in Newaygo with Trent."

"I so honor you for saying that."

"I know we loved each other and that was wonderful . . . but sometimes it was really hard."

"I'm sure."

"Especially after Jenna left. He would go out into the woods with his gun . . ."

"Even though you loved each other, you had this beautiful love, you still had to be watching all the time, alert for something going wrong."

Sometimes a tear will come out one eye and then the other. This time they were coming out both eyes, fast. The lump in my throat kept me from speaking.

Elaine continued. "Trent experienced joy with you, for one of the few times in his life, being with you and being with you in Newaygo. But there was a part of him that could not be healed. His parents—rightly he had anger toward his parents, toward his father for the physical brutality; but in some ways, what his mother did was much worse. Trent was never able to direct that anger at the people who deserved it. Instead, he took it inside and directed it at himself."

I held on to the quilt and listened to Elaine with wet eyes.

"Even though you created this space to love each other, there was still for Trent this pain. If he had asked me when it was going to stop, I would have told him, 'Never. It's never going to stop. You are going to need to learn to live around the pain.'"

As she said this, Elaine made a fist with one hand and the other flew in the air around it.

I swallowed the lump and asked, "Do you think he died because he knew I was wearing out?"

"No. Oh, no. He had hoped that when he got to Newaygo it would get better. But it never got better. I believe there are some traumas that are so great that healing is not possible."

I agreed with her and said so, that if it is true in the medical world that sometimes a physical body goes past the point of recovery, it makes sense that it would be true of the psychological body as well.

Elaine and I always hug each other at the beginning and end of a session. At the beginning I had hugged her strongly and almost lifted her off the ground. Now I gave a good hug but a weak hug because I was spent. I had told Elaine my secret.

I don't know how long I would have lasted in Newaygo with Trent.

Perfect Time

The lease on the Newaygo storage locker that holds items marked with blue tape is up in November. Jenna has fallen in love and moved with her boyfriend to another state. I don't think she'll come back for whatever is still in there, so I'm planning on making one last trip, probably in April, when the Muskegon River is high and fast.

I miss kayaking and there are times, still, when I miss Trent. We had our mantra in Newaygo and I have my mantra for the life I live now. "He died at the perfect time" is what I say to myself whenever I start to think he should still be with me, still beside me, his blue eyes looking back at me when I wake up in the morning. "He died at the perfect time" is the short version. The long version is, "I don't know what good things may happen because of this. I don't know everything there is to know about this. I do know that he doesn't have headaches anymore. I do know that he loves me." He told me this. He told me he would love me forever.

He died at the perfect time.

Sweet baby, I just talked to you. I love you so much. Baby, the love I have for you is so huge you can't see it in one day. So I'm going to show you a little piece of it every day for the rest of my life and there's going to be so much left that you'll see it for eternity. I love you.

—Trent Price

Acknowledgments

It takes a village to raise a child and to birth a book. These thanks go to some of the many people who helped give birth to this one.

Thank you to those who instigated and supported writing that could be read by others:

Seth Godin, who with his books and his blog and his tribe made me realize that the tools of production are in our hands and who made me want to start a blog. He is my Zig.

Deb Freuh, Laurie Anderson, and Linda Rasins, the three other women of LLDJ, who, when I told them I wanted to start a blog about adult learning said, "No. Write about Trent."

Megan Elizabeth Morris, the blog architect.

Paul Calhoun, the builder of elegant code.

Kathy Bussert of DesignSpring, the artist.

The readers who let me know by their comments that I wasn't just blogging into the wind: Becky Blanton, Bernd Nurnberger, Bolaji Oyejide, Chris Brogan, Darren Scott Monroe, Deb Freuh, Didier Daglinckx, Frances Schagen, Georgia Kohlbeck, Georgianne Carli, Ginger Blackwell, Igor Asselbergs, Jenna Price, Jodi Kaplan, Judy Vorfeld, Kayla Lamoreaux, Kendra Cribley, Kyle Zelazny, Laura Hicks, Lia Scomazzon, Linda Rasins, Marcos Gaser, Mark Bottemiller, Mary Rose Maguire, Megan Elizabeth Morris, Paul Calhoun, Rahul Deodhar, Rita Johnson,

Rosemary Marx, Rupa, Shanna Mann, Sue Canfield, Susan Finerty, Tom Bentley, Ujjwal Trivedi.

Thank you to those who helped the blog become a book:

Helen Glenn Court, development editor, who wielded her red pen like an X-Acto knife and turned a collection of stories into a compelling narrative. Without Glenn's work, people would have stopped reading by chapter four. Or page four.

Carolyn Haley, copy editor, who removed stumbling blocks from the reader's experience.

Lori Paximadis, proofing editor, who made sure all was as it should be.

Those who read early drafts, who made comments and asked questions that led to improvements in writing, continuity, and structure: Bernd Nurnberger, Deb Freuh, Elaine Kulp, Didier Daglinckx, Georgia Kohlbeck, Georgianne Carli, Ginger Blackwell, Igor Asselbergs, Judy Vorfeld, Laura Cison, Laurie Anderson, Lia Scomazzon, Linda Rasins, Marcos Gaser, Mary Rose Maguire, Rosemary Marx, Sabine Hägele, Shanna Mann, Susan Finerty.

JMJ at crowdSPRING, who kept reworking the cover as it went from on the ground to under the ground to into the sky. Jelena, thank you for your dedication to the evolution. I love it.

JohnBlaine at crowdSPRING, who designed the Poppyseed House logo, and who was spot on with the first draft. I love it.

Igor Asselbergs at Colorjinn, who gave his color expertise to the cover.

Guido Henkel, who created the ebook versions.

Elke Sigal, who led by example.

The resources that helped me know what to do:

APE: Author, Publisher, Entrepreneur, by Guy Kawasaki.

The Naked Truth About Self-Publishing, by Jana DeLeon, Tina Folsom, Colleen Gleason and Jane Graves.

The Non-Designer's Design Book, by Robin Williams.

Butterick's Practical Typography, by Matthew Butterick.

Joel Friedlander's blog at www.thebookdesigner.com

Expanding the circle of appreciation to those who make it possible for me to write:

Fifth Third Bank, which has given me a job I love more than any I've ever held, and which enables me to write without worrying about paying the bills.

Krystyna, who tends to my home. One of my great pleasures is getting into my bed on a day when she has been there. The sheets are fresh and it feels like getting into a hug.

Manoj and Natu, who take me to and from the airport and who are exemplars of customer service. When I apologize to Manoj for needing to pick me up at 3:45 a.m., he brushes it aside with, "You are my personal customer." And when I text Natu, asking if he can pick me up, his response is always, "Yes. I will take care of you." They do.

David Lipman of Home Alone Pet Care and the fine folks at Morton Grove Animal Hospital who watch over Leda when I am out of town and who allow me to relax, knowing that she is in good hands.

Expanding the circle still further, there are those who shape the book and those who shape the author:

My parents, those first shapers of who I am, who each taught me important and different lessons. Special thanks to my mother, who read to me every night for years, which led to my love of books. Thank you also for standing up to my first grade teacher who thought I shouldn't cry when hearing a story by asking, "Do you think it's sad when Bambi's mother dies?"

Miss Ploughman, who opened up the world of learning and made me feel safe, special, and loved. Thank you, thank you, thank you.

Dr. Gary McLean, who fostered my creativity, and who floored me when he used the word "brilliant."

The women of the dedication: Denise Broz, Elaine Kulp, Ginger Blackwell, Kendra Cribley, Laura Cison, Laurie Anderson, Linda Rasins, Sabine Hägele. You are the sisters I never had.

Trent Allen Price, who adored me and who said, "True stories are the best kind." I love you, I miss you, and I'm looking forward to seeing you . . . but not yet.

Jule Kucera, May 2013

Jule Kucera has been writing for two decades in the corporate world and blogging since 2009. She lives in Chicagoland with her sweet rescued greyhound Leda, surrounded by many friends. This is her first book.

CPSIA information can be obtained
at www.ICGtesting.com
Printed in the USA
LVHW040055110419
613764LV00001B/167

9 780990 455509